Incredible Plants

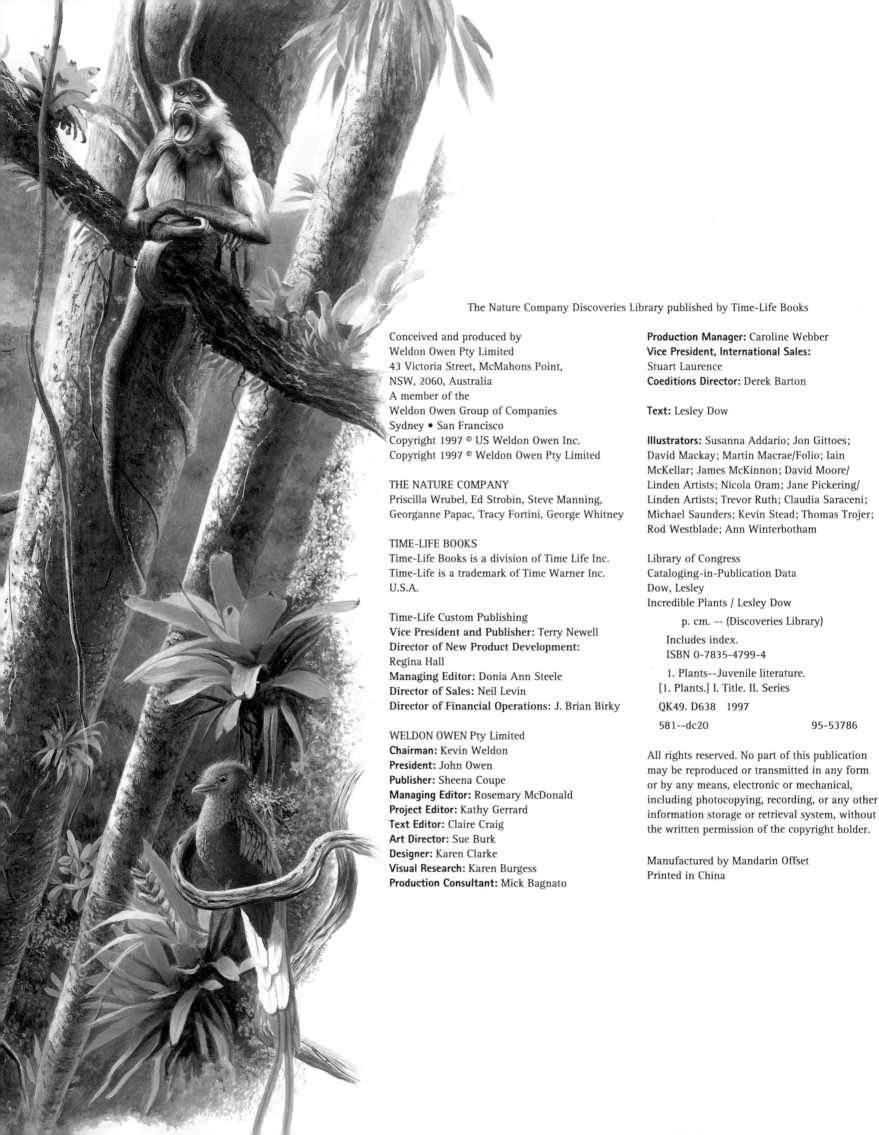

The Nature Company Discoveries Library published by Time-Life Books

Conceived and produced by
Weldon Owen Pty Limited
43 Victoria Street, McMahons Point,
NSW, 2060, Australia
A member of the
Weldon Owen Group of Companies
Sydney • San Francisco
Copyright 1997 © US Weldon Owen Inc.
Copyright 1997 © Weldon Owen Pty Limited

THE NATURE COMPANY
Priscilla Wrubel, Ed Strobin, Steve Manning,
Georganne Papac, Tracy Fortini, George Whitney

TIME-LIFE BOOKS
Time-Life Books is a division of Time Life Inc.
Time-Life is a trademark of Time Warner Inc.
U.S.A.

Time-Life Custom Publishing
Vice President and Publisher: Terry Newell
Director of New Product Development:
Regina Hall
Managing Editor: Donia Ann Steele
Director of Sales: Neil Levin
Director of Financial Operations: J. Brian Birky

WELDON OWEN Pty Limited
Chairman: Kevin Weldon
President: John Owen
Publisher: Sheena Coupe
Managing Editor: Rosemary McDonald
Project Editor: Kathy Gerrard
Text Editor: Claire Craig
Art Director: Sue Burk
Designer: Karen Clarke
Visual Research: Karen Burgess
Production Consultant: Mick Bagnato

Production Manager: Caroline Webber
Vice President, International Sales:
Stuart Laurence
Coeditions Director: Derek Barton

Text: Lesley Dow

Illustrators: Susanna Addario; Jon Gittoes;
David Mackay; Martin Macrae/Folio; Iain
McKellar; James McKinnon; David Moore/
Linden Artists; Nicola Oram; Jane Pickering/
Linden Artists; Trevor Ruth; Claudia Saraceni;
Michael Saunders; Kevin Stead; Thomas Trojer;
Rod Westblade; Ann Winterbotham

Library of Congress
Cataloging-in-Publication Data
Dow, Lesley
Incredible Plants / Lesley Dow

p. cm. -- (Discoveries Library)

Includes index.
ISBN 0-7835-4799-4

1. Plants--Juvenile literature.
[1. Plants.] I. Title. II. Series

QK49. D638   1997

581--dc20   95-53786

Manufactured by Mandarin Offset
Printed in China

THE NATURE COMPANY
DISCOVERIES
LIBRARY

Incredible Plants

CONSULTING EDITOR

Dr. Roger Carolin
Formerly Associate Professor of Biology,
University of Sydney,
Australia

TIME
LIFE
BOOKS

Contents

• UNDERSTANDING PLANTS •

• THE PLANT KINGDOM •

• WHERE PLANTS LIVE •

• PLANTS AND HUMANS •

Introducing Plants

Plants are the key to the survival of all other living things. Plants provide much of the oxygen that animals and humans breathe, as well as much of the food they eat. Scientists who study plants, called botanists, have found and described more than 350,000 types of plants, but there are more. Plants come in all sizes and shapes. Some are so tiny you cannot see them without a microscope, but some are so tall you can scarcely see the top of them without a telescope. Many plants have brilliantly colored flowers and others have no flowers at all. Plants look different because they live in very different environments—on land or in water, thick forests or open plains, freezing mountains or hot deserts. Over millions of years, they have adapted to suit their own environment.

MICROSCOPIC VIEW
This tiny, single-celled diatom is one of the simplest plants. Its ancestors grew during the time of the dinosaurs. It could take up to 50 diatoms to cover the period at the end of this sentence.

ALL SHAPES AND SIZES
Plants grow in almost every environment in the world. Their size, shape and the way they grow are designed so that they can get the essential water and energy they need to survive, wherever they grow.

PLANT CELL

All living things are made up of microscopic cells and each cell has its own special function or purpose. Most cells contain a nucleus (the genetic control center) and a number of mitochondria that convert sugars into energy. They float in a liquid jelly called cytoplasm. Only plant cells, however, have chloroplasts. These contain chlorophyll, which is used in making the plant's food supply. Plant cells are also the only cells that have firm walls made of cellulose.

Group of plant cells

Single plant cell

Chloroplast

Cell wall

Nucleus

Cytoplasm

Mitochondria

PLANT PROFILE
Plants make their own food and have hard cell walls made of cellulose. They never stop growing and are usually rooted to one place.

DID YOU KNOW?

Most plants keep on growing until they die. Other living creatures stop growing when they reach maturity or become adults. Humans usually stop growing in their late teens or early twenties. Can you imagine how tall you would be at 80 if you kept on growing?

Plant Parts

Unlike single-celled green algae (left), most plants have hundreds, thousands or even millions of cells. Plant cells are highly organized, and each part of a plant has its own specialized group of cells. Flowering plants have four parts: roots, stems, leaves and flowers. The roots, stems and leaves all contain xylem, the specialized transporting tissue that carries water and mineral salts, and phloem, which carries the nutrients (food) the plant makes. Each part of the plant has a different task. The roots anchor the plant and draw up water and mineral salts from the soil. The stem holds the plant up towards the light and transports water, mineral salts and other nutrients to the rest of the plant. The leaves make food for the whole plant and provide most of the breathing holes. The flowers contain the reproductive organs. The plant can survive only if the four parts do the jobs they are designed to do efficiently.

ATTRACTING INSECTS
Rose petals may look smooth, but under a microscope you can see special light-reflecting cells that make the petals colorful and attractive to insects.

Xylem

Phloem

STEM SUPPORT
The xylem in the stem transports water and mineral salts up to the leaves and flowers. The phloem transports nutrients up or down to wherever they are needed.

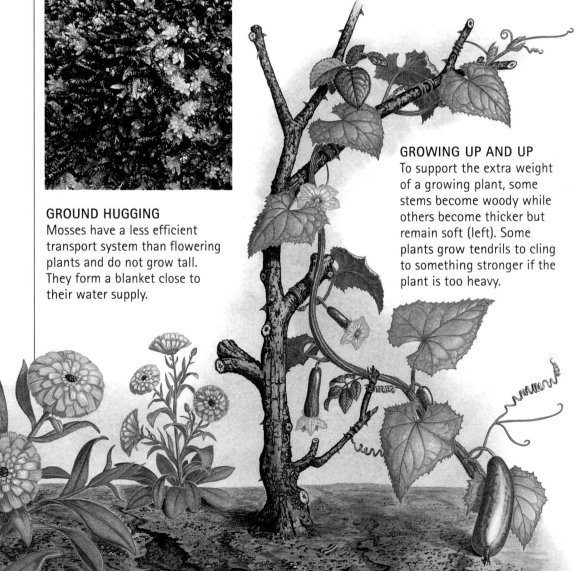

GROUND HUGGING
Mosses have a less efficient transport system than flowering plants and do not grow tall. They form a blanket close to their water supply.

GROWING UP AND UP
To support the extra weight of a growing plant, some stems become woody while others become thicker but remain soft (left). Some plants grow tendrils to cling to something stronger if the plant is too heavy.

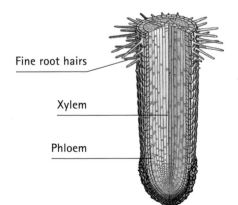

Fine root hairs

Xylem

Phloem

GATHERING SUPPLIES
Fine hairs on the tip of the root absorb water and mineral salts from the soil. These flow up the xylem like milk up a straw. Nutrients that provide energy travel down to the roots through the phloem.

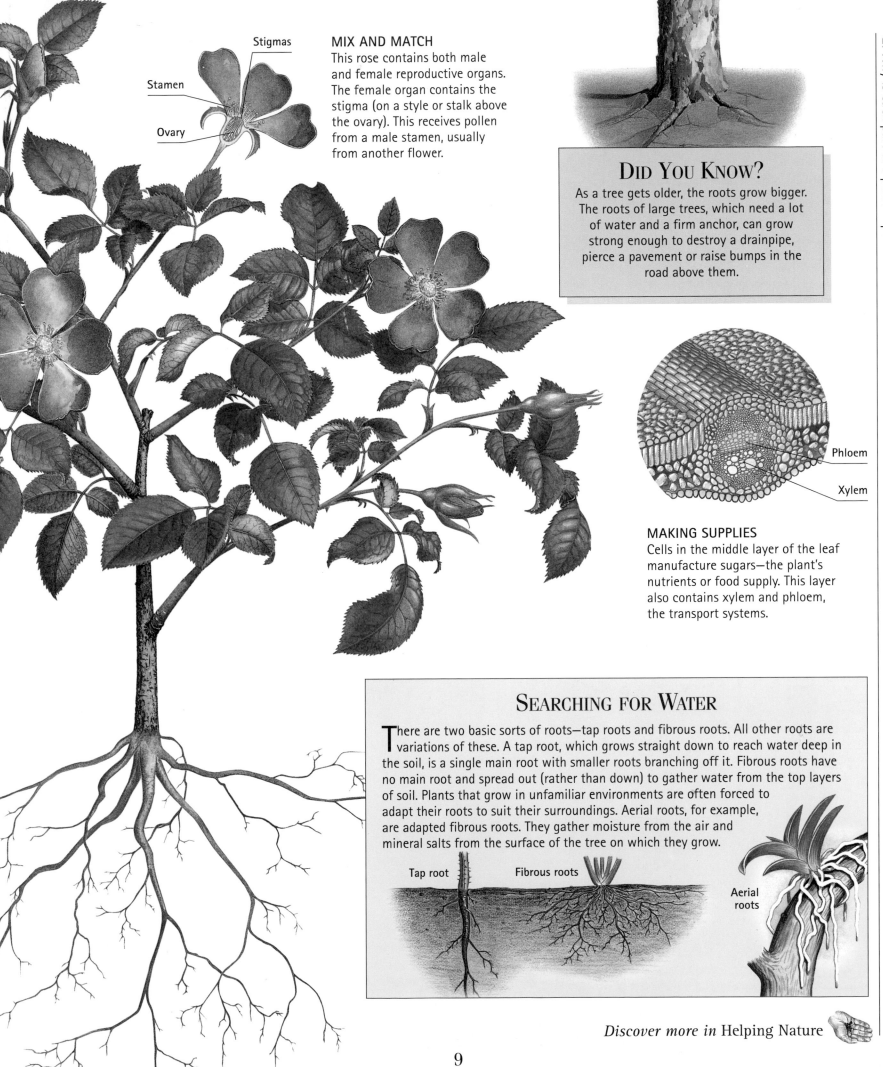

MIX AND MATCH
This rose contains both male and female reproductive organs. The female organ contains the stigma (on a style or stalk above the ovary). This receives pollen from a male stamen, usually from another flower.

Stigmas

Stamen

Ovary

DID YOU KNOW?
As a tree gets older, the roots grow bigger. The roots of large trees, which need a lot of water and a firm anchor, can grow strong enough to destroy a drainpipe, pierce a pavement or raise bumps in the road above them.

Phloem

Xylem

MAKING SUPPLIES
Cells in the middle layer of the leaf manufacture sugars—the plant's nutrients or food supply. This layer also contains xylem and phloem, the transport systems.

SEARCHING FOR WATER
There are two basic sorts of roots—tap roots and fibrous roots. All other roots are variations of these. A tap root, which grows straight down to reach water deep in the soil, is a single main root with smaller roots branching off it. Fibrous roots have no main root and spread out (rather than down) to gather water from the top layers of soil. Plants that grow in unfamiliar environments are often forced to adapt their roots to suit their surroundings. Aerial roots, for example, are adapted fibrous roots. They gather moisture from the air and mineral salts from the surface of the tree on which they grow.

Tap root

Fibrous roots

Aerial roots

Discover more in Helping Nature

Plant Processes

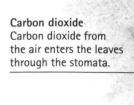

Animals must go out and find food, but most plants stand still and make their own. Their food-making process is called photosynthesis and it uses four ingredients: daylight (*photos* in Greek), chlorophyll to absorb or trap the light, water and mineral salts from the soil, and carbon dioxide from the air. Chlorophyll is found only in the green part of plants. This is usually the leaves, but in some plants, like the cactus (above), most of the chlorophyll is found in the stem. From these ingredients, the plant manufactures sugars and, in the process, gives off oxygen. Some of this oxygen is used by the plant in another process called respiration. In dark and daylight hours, this process converts the sugars into the energy the plant needs to live and grow. Most of the oxygen, however, returns to the air and is the source of the vital oxygen that we breathe.

Carbon dioxide
Carbon dioxide from the air enters the leaves through the stomata.

Oxygen and water
Oxygen, a by-product of photosynthesis, and excess water are released into the air.

THE RECYCLING PLANT
The leaves absorb sunlight and "breathe in" carbon dioxide. The roots absorb water and mineral salts, which the xylem transports to the leaves. The chlorophyll now has all it needs to make the sugars, which the phloem transports around the plant.

UPSIDE-DOWN LEAVES
The stomata in most plants are on the underside of the leaves. In these lily pads the stomata are on the upper side, facing the air, because this is their source of carbon dioxide (for photosynthesis).

SAVING WATER
As water is lost through the leaves in a process called transpiration, some trees shed their leaves in the coldest or driest season. The tree survives on stored food and the leaves fertilize the soil around the roots.

DID YOU KNOW?
As seaweeds produce food through photosynthesis, they need green chlorophyll. In red and brown seaweeds, the green chlorophyll is hidden by the stronger colors of "assistant" pigments. These help the chlorophyll to absorb the sunlight passing through water.

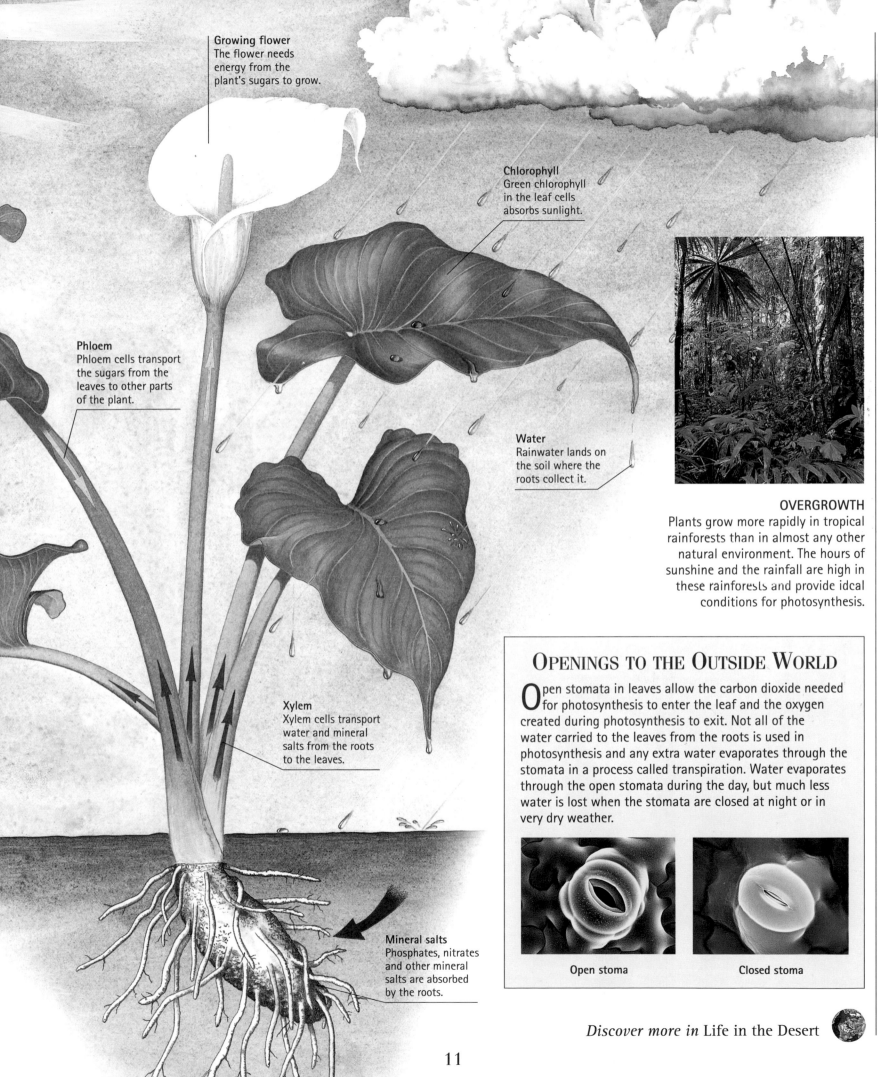

Growing flower
The flower needs energy from the plant's sugars to grow.

Chlorophyll
Green chlorophyll in the leaf cells absorbs sunlight.

Phloem
Phloem cells transport the sugars from the leaves to other parts of the plant.

Water
Rainwater lands on the soil where the roots collect it.

Xylem
Xylem cells transport water and mineral salts from the roots to the leaves.

Mineral salts
Phosphates, nitrates and other mineral salts are absorbed by the roots.

OVERGROWTH
Plants grow more rapidly in tropical rainforests than in almost any other natural environment. The hours of sunshine and the rainfall are high in these rainforests and provide ideal conditions for photosynthesis.

OPENINGS TO THE OUTSIDE WORLD

Open stomata in leaves allow the carbon dioxide needed for photosynthesis to enter the leaf and the oxygen created during photosynthesis to exit. Not all of the water carried to the leaves from the roots is used in photosynthesis and any extra water evaporates through the stomata in a process called transpiration. Water evaporates through the open stomata during the day, but much less water is lost when the stomata are closed at night or in very dry weather.

Open stoma

Closed stoma

Discover more in Life in the Desert

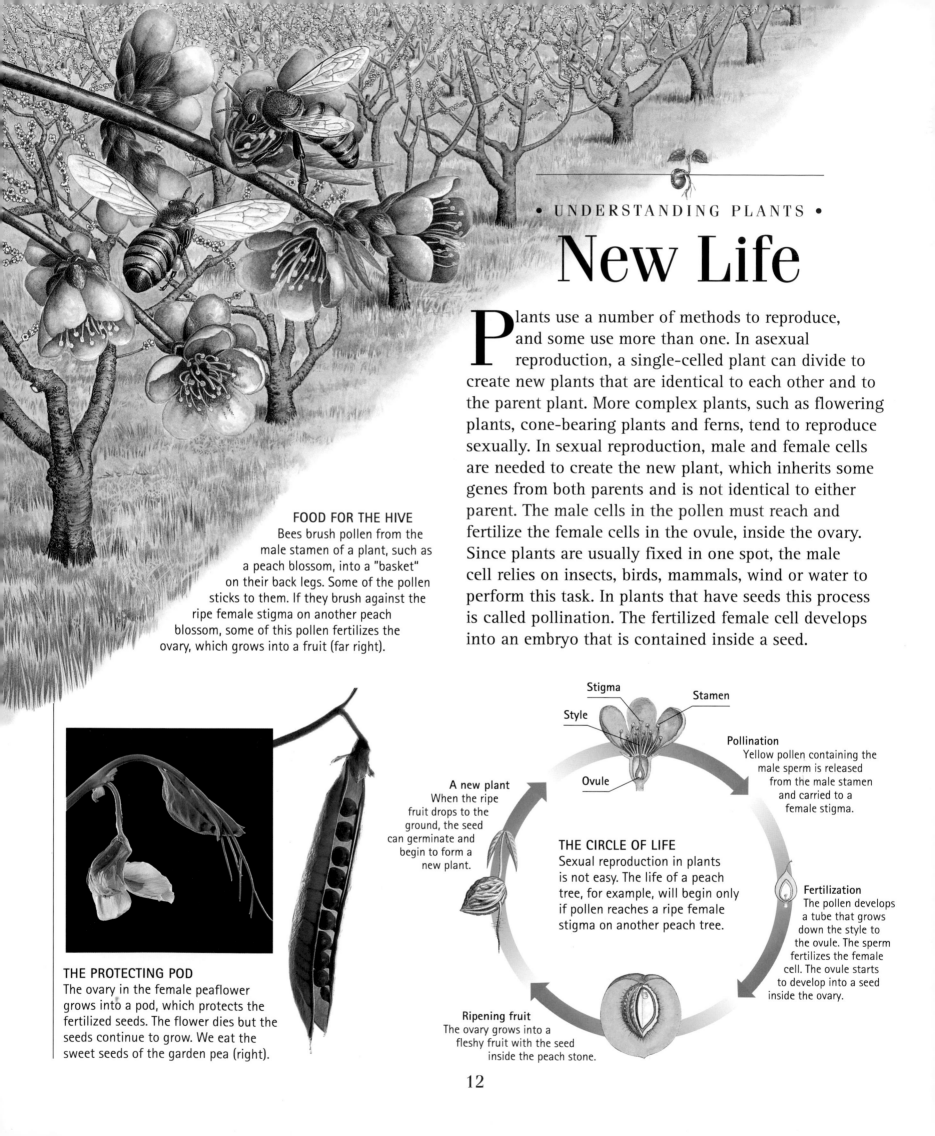

New Life

Plants use a number of methods to reproduce, and some use more than one. In asexual reproduction, a single-celled plant can divide to create new plants that are identical to each other and to the parent plant. More complex plants, such as flowering plants, cone-bearing plants and ferns, tend to reproduce sexually. In sexual reproduction, male and female cells are needed to create the new plant, which inherits some genes from both parents and is not identical to either parent. The male cells in the pollen must reach and fertilize the female cells in the ovule, inside the ovary. Since plants are usually fixed in one spot, the male cell relies on insects, birds, mammals, wind or water to perform this task. In plants that have seeds this process is called pollination. The fertilized female cell develops into an embryo that is contained inside a seed.

FOOD FOR THE HIVE
Bees brush pollen from the male stamen of a plant, such as a peach blossom, into a "basket" on their back legs. Some of the pollen sticks to them. If they brush against the ripe female stigma on another peach blossom, some of this pollen fertilizes the ovary, which grows into a fruit (far right).

THE PROTECTING POD
The ovary in the female peaflower grows into a pod, which protects the fertilized seeds. The flower dies but the seeds continue to grow. We eat the sweet seeds of the garden pea (right).

Stigma

Stamen

Style

Ovule

Pollination
Yellow pollen containing the male sperm is released from the male stamen and carried to a female stigma.

A new plant
When the ripe fruit drops to the ground, the seed can germinate and begin to form a new plant.

THE CIRCLE OF LIFE
Sexual reproduction in plants is not easy. The life of a peach tree, for example, will begin only if pollen reaches a ripe female stigma on another peach tree.

Fertilization
The pollen develops a tube that grows down the style to the ovule. The sperm fertilizes the female cell. The ovule starts to develop into a seed inside the ovary.

Ripening fruit
The ovary grows into a fleshy fruit with the seed inside the peach stone.

12

DID YOU KNOW?

Not all fruits have a fleshy layer like a peach does. Each flower on a yellow dandelion has an ovary that grows into a fruit with a single seed. The fruit, with a stalk capped by feathery hairs, is light enough to be blown by you, or the wind.

CHOICES

This colony of volvox (simple single-celled algae) can reproduce asexually by releasing new colonies into the water (as shown), or sexually by releasing male sperm and female ova.

REPRODUCING WITHOUT SEEDS

Some plants can grow, or propagate, identical plants from their stems or roots. They can also provide water and food for the new plant until its own roots and leaves grow. Many ferns have underground horizontal stems, called rhizomes, which divide and produce identical plants. Daffodil bulbs split and grow new bulbs on the side of the parent bulb. Strawberries send out horizontal stems or runners above the ground. A new strawberry plant grows where the part of the runner with small leaves, called the node, reaches the ground.

Fern

Daffodil bulb

Strawberry

NAKED SEEDS

Each scale on this female cone protects two seeds without ovaries. They are fertilized by pollen from a smaller male cone. When the scales open, the winged seeds fall gently to the ground.

TWO STAGES

Fern spores, on the underside of fronds, drop to the ground and grow into a new plant that produces male and female gametes, or sex cells. If these cells unite, a new spore-producing fern will grow.

Discover more in Plants with Spores

13

Germination and Growth

Once a plant seed is fertilized, it needs to find a suitable patch of ground, where the light, moisture and temperature are right, in order to grow. Directly underneath the parent tree, which would shade it from the light and whose bigger roots would compete for water, is not an ideal position. Plants use various methods to make sure their seeds reach good growing ground. Some plants scatter their own seeds and others rely on wind, water or animals. Not all of these seeds start growing immediately, and some never begin to grow at all. Inside the seed casing is a supply of food that allows the seed to wait for days, months or even years until conditions are right for germination. Then the first tiny shoot and root break through the seed case. After an initial period of growth, which in some plants may last days and in others years, the plant matures and can reproduce.

GONE WITH THE WIND
The fruits of the thistle have a parachute of hairs. They are light enough for the wind to carry them long distances. With luck, some will find the right environment in which to germinate.

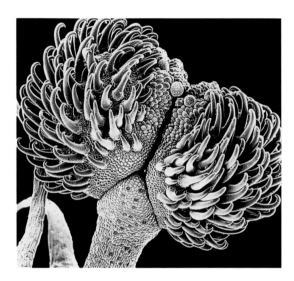

HOOKED
Check your clothes and the dog's fur next time you go for a walk. Some seeds, like the goosegrass, have tiny hooks that latch on to animals or humans and are moved to a new location.

HARDWORKING HELPERS
The gathering instincts of ants are very useful for plants. Ants collect seeds for food and move them from one place to another. Some of the uneaten seeds will germinate in fertile soil.

THE BUOYANT COCONUT
The coconuts that fall from palm trees are often carried by water to a suitable growing environment. A new coconut palm may grow and produce its own fruits.

Washed ashore
A coconut, with the seed inside, floats on water and can travel many miles from its parent tree before it reaches land.

BUILT TO FLY
Like tiny whirling helicopters, maple seeds spin in the wind and land gently. If not eaten by animals and birds, the seeds may take root and start to grow.

DID YOU KNOW?
Some fruits explode to scatter their seeds away from the shade of the parent plant. Squirting cucumbers, dwarf mistletoe and Himalayan balsam shoot out seeds at up to 46 ft (14 m) per second.

CATCHING THE LIGHT

Leaves and sunlight are needed to make food for the new plant to grow. Leaves may grow singly off the stem, in pairs from the same point (node) on the stem, or in groups. But if you look at them from above, the way the sun shines on them, the leaves are all at different angles from each other in a spiral shape. Each leaf has some of its surface facing the sun and is not shaded by the leaf above it.

SWALLOWED WHOLE
Fruit bats, birds and other animals eat many seeds without killing them. The seeds travel in the animal's gut inside their seed casings, which can survive digestive juices. Then they are passed out—still whole—in the animal's droppings.

When the time is ripe
The embryo is dormant in the seed but when conditions are suitable, it feeds on the coconut milk and sends out the first stem and root.

Breaking out
As the roots take in water and the stem grows stronger, the outer shell breaks open.

The second generation
The coconut tree will drop its own fruits. These will be washed out to sea and begin their own long voyage to germination.

15

Carboniferous: 362–290 million years ago
Giant horsetails, club mosses, ferns and cordaitales,
as well as giant amphibians and dragonflies, appeared.

Permian: 290–245 million years ago
Seed-bearing gingkoes and conifers thrived.
Mammal-like reptiles appeared.

Triassic: 245–208 million years ago
Cycads flourished, cordaitales became
extinct. Meat-eating dinosaurs appeared.

• THE PLANT KINGDOM •

Plant Beginnings

The Earth's crust is 4,600 million years old, but for more than 1,000 million years only non-living things, such as rocks and water, could exist because of the poisonous gases in the atmosphere and the fierce heat of the sun. The first true plants grew in the nutrient-rich oceans about 550 million years ago and the first land plants appeared 400 million years ago. As these primitive land plants did not have a water-transport system, they grew near lakes. They were the ancestors of the spore-bearing plants—the giant club mosses, horsetails and ferns (fossilized fern above left) that formed huge forests during the Carboniferous Period. Seed-bearing plants, such as conifers, which appeared 350 million years ago, and flowering plants, which appeared only 135 million years ago, contributed to dinosaurs' food and oxygen supplies. Unlike the dinosaurs, however, plants did not become extinct when many animal species did, 65 million years ago.

Swampy Carboniferous
Giant club mosses (1), giant horsetails (2) and cordaitales (3) grew as tall as houses.

Cooler Permian
Gingkoes (4) and conifers (5) shared the world with other early plants.

Drier Triassic
Cycads (6) flourished.

Cooler and wetter Jurassic
New species of conifers, such as swamp cypress (7) and monkey puzzle (8), appeared in the lush, ferny undergrowth (9).

Flowering Cretaceous
Flowering plants, such as bulrushes (10), magnolia bushes (11) and willow trees (12) appeared.

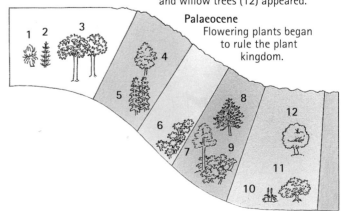

Palaeocene
Flowering plants began to rule the plant kingdom.

16

PLANTS ON LAND

Over millions of years, different plants—spore-bearing plants, cone-bearing plants and flowering plants—have dominated the Earth. Climate affected plant and animal life. The plants shown here grew in a cold climate in the Northern Hemisphere.

LIVING FOSSILS

These stromatolites in Western Australia are spongy structures created by layers of blue-green algae and mud that are shaped by waves and currents. They are usually found only as fossils, some of which date back 3,500 million years.

A SLIMY SURVIVOR

The next time you see dark slime in a fish tank or slip on some on a wet path, you should be amazed rather than annoyed. The slime is made up of chains of single-celled blue-green algae or cyanobacteria. Like bacteria, they have no roots, stems or leaves but, like plants, they produce oxygen during photosynthesis. Blue-green algae are the earliest known life forms and have survived for 3,500 million years in watery environments as extreme as Arctic pack ice and boiling hot springs.

Q: What lived on the Earth 4,600 million years ago?

Jurassic: 208–145 million years ago
New species of conifer appeared. Long-necked dinosaurs, plated dinosaurs and flying reptiles appeared.

Cretaceous: 145–65 million years ago
Flowering plants, including trees, appeared. Horned dinosaurs and snakes appeared.

Palaeocene: 65–56 million years ago
Flowering plants dominated. Dinosaurs disappeared and small mammals appeared.

The First Plants

Algae, the world's first plants, are even more different from each other than roses are from palm trees. Among the 25,000 species there are single-celled green slime, freshwater weed and huge brown or red seaweed. But they do have some things in common. They grow only where there is water, and this includes the underside of whales, snowfields and desert soils. They have no true roots, stems or leaves but they do have green chlorophyll and manufacture their food supplies by photosynthesis. Algae have no seeds and reproduce by dividing or breaking off cells, by releasing spores from spore cases in their fronds or, sexually, by releasing male and female cells. All of these methods require water and, when the first green algal colonies reached land, their methods of reproduction gradually adapted to a less reliable water supply. Algae now share the world with their more complex seed-bearing descendants.

CHAMPION GROWER
Giant kelp grows extremely quickly—up to 12 in (30 cm) a day! As tall as rainforest trees, giant kelp forms dense canopies or ocean forests. These provide shelter, food and oxygen for sea creatures.

POISONOUS EXPLOSION
Millions of blue-green algae together can form a huge colored tide that you can see from space. This algal tide, or bloom, suffocates or poisons the fish that usually feed on algae.

GREEN SLIME
Seen under a microscope, pond spirogyra has long chains of identical cells. It can reproduce asexually, when the long chains break into pieces that form new plants, or sexually, when cells from different chains fuse.

LIVING TOGETHER
Lichen is not a single, independently growing plant but is the result of close cooperation between an alga and a fungus (below left). The alga provides the food, and the fungus wrapped around it provides shelter and minerals. Lichens grow very slowly—0.04 in (1 mm) a year—but can live for up to 4,000 years. They are the hardiest of all plants and can survive on rocks in sunbaked deserts, high in the Himalayas or in the freezing Arctic.

Fungus and alga   Rainforest lichen

Food-producing fronds
The waving fronds provide the kelp's food through photosynthesis and release their spores into the water in spring.

Buoyant bladders
Filled with gas, the giant kelp's bladders hold the fronds afloat, nearer to the surface and the sunlight.

MAKING AIR
These bubbles show that algae produce oxygen during photosynthesis. Other sea dwellers need this oxygen to live. Since oceans cover a large part of the Earth's surface, algae are also a major source of the oxygen we breathe.

Hanging on
The holdfast clings to the ocean bedrock and, like the rest of the plant, absorbs water and mineral salts from the sea.

Plants with Spores

Ferns, mosses, liverworts and hornworts produce spores in order to reproduce. A spore is a tiny specialised cell that is able to grow into an organism. These plants are more primitive and reproduce less efficiently than plants that produce seeds. Mosses, liverworts and hornworts are descended from algae. They have no true roots, stems or transport systems. They form low-growing mats in damp places to get water directly from their environment. The 20,000 and more species of moss and liverwort have not evolved into other kinds of plants and have no descendants. Ferns, club mosses and horsetails have adapted better to life on land. They can grow tall and get a better share of the light because they developed roots, stems and transport systems for water and nutrients. Millions of years ago, their larger ancestors were the most dominant plants on Earth. Today, however, it is the turn of seed-producing plants to dominate the plant kingdom.

A FERN SELECTION
Elkhorn (top) and crow's-nest ferns grow on trees without harming them. Rasp fern (bottom) reproduces rapidly from its horizontal stems. Tree ferns (far right) can grow as tall as palm trees but the delicate maidenhair below them stays close to the ground.

Breaking out
When the spore case opens, the spores scatter in the wind.

Asexual spores
Spores have no sex cells and form in spore cases (sporangia) on the underside of the fern's fronds.

THREE GENERATIONS
Ferns have a unique life cycle. The first generation produces asexual spores, the second generation produces sex cells, or gametes, and these grow into a third generation of spore producers.

Gametes
The spore grows into a tiny plant called a gametophyte because it has male and female sex cells, or gametes.

A new spore producer
The male cell needs at least a film of water to swim to and join the female cell before a new spore-producing fern can grow.

COPY CONE

Club mosses are related to ferns, not mosses. They have special spore-carrying leaves that grow in tight spirals. These leaves protect the spore cases and look like cones.

MOSS SPORES

The spearlike stalk with its spore capsule grows on a moss parent plant until it ripens. The hood falls off and the spore capsule releases its tiny spores through "teeth" at the top of the capsule.

WATER CATCHER

Mosses and liverworts need water to survive and to produce the next generation, but they have no roots to trap water and no xylem to transport it inside the plant. They must use other means to trap water. This *Frullania* liverwort, which grows on trees in a dry environment, has an ingenious water-trapping system. Small "flasks" form on the primitive "leaves" and catch water running down the tree trunk. The water can then trickle to other parts of the plant.

Flask

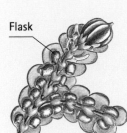

Microscopic view of *Frullania*

Moist *Frullania*

THE GREATEST SOAKER

Sphagnum moss can soak up 20 times its own weight in water. This soggy carpet grows in acid water with few bacteria so it is sterile enough to be used as an emergency bandage. When sphagnum moss is dried and partly decomposed, it forms peat—a household fuel in some countries.

SURVIVORS

The horsetail's whorls of green branches and hollow stem work together to produce the plant's food. The leaves, which are the brownish-black scales pressed tightly against the stem, are not food producers. Horsetail spores, grouped into cones, grow on separate stems.

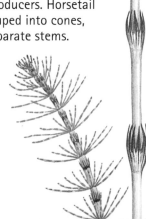

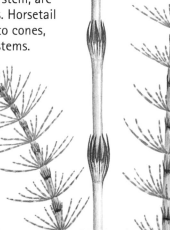

Gingko
Female gingko trees have fleshy, foul-smelling cones and fan-shaped leaves.

Yew
Yew leaves are narrow and flat. Female yew seeds are a fleshy red.

Scots pine
Scots pines have egg-shaped cones and paired, blue-green leaves.

Arizona cypress
Dark green overlapping leaves cover each cypress twig, like scales. The cones are small and round.

Cycad
Cycad cones are the largest cones in the world. They grow in a crown of spiky fronds.

Plum Pine
Plum pines have berry-like cones with a fleshy seed stalk sticking out.

Conifers and Their Relatives

TWO CONES
Male and female cones can grow on the same or a different tree. The pollen needed for fertilizing the female cell is inside each scale of the smaller male cone.

Seed-bearing plants evolved 50 million years after the first land plants. Their seeds grew inside cones, not inside fruits. Today the largest group of cone bearers are the conifers—pines, spruces, firs, cypresses and their relatives. Most have hard, woody male and female cones, although a few species have fleshy cones. The tough-skinned leaves of many conifers are like green needles or like scales pressed flat against the branch. They are called evergreen trees because they do not shed their leaves all at the same time. Conifers grow fast in forests in cool, temperate climates. Their wood is soft and easy to work with so they are planted in commercial forests, often in places where they would not grow naturally. Cone-bearing cycads, gingkoes, yews and the unusual desert welwitschia are distantly related to the true conifers.

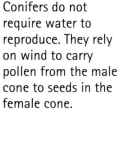

A burst of yellow dust
In spring, the male pine cone releases millions of pollen grains. A few days later, the male cone drops off the tree. Its job is finished.

ODD ONE OUT
In spring and summer, larches have green leaves. These leaves change color in autumn and drop off in winter, which is unusual for a conifer.

CONIFER CYCLE
Conifers do not require water to reproduce. They rely on wind to carry pollen from the male cone to seeds in the female cone.

Germination
If the seed finds a spot with enough warmth, moisture and light, it germinates and a new conifer grows.

Sticky cone
The pollen lands on a sticky female cone. A pollen tube starts to grow and, up to a year later, the sperm finally fertilizes the ovule.

Swelling cone
The female cone grows to four times its size as the seeds grow inside. Two years later when the seeds are mature, the cone opens to release them.

Spreading seeds
Each seed has a wing and can take off in the wind. It also has food for germination inside a tough, outer casing.

INSIDE A TREE TRUNK

The outer bark of a tree is made up of dead phloem cells but the inner bark is spongy and living. New cells grow between the phloem, or bark layer, on the outside and xylem, or wood layer, on the inside. This is why a tree trunk gets wider every year. The xylem rings—one for each year of growth—tell how old the tree is. The V shapes in these rings show where branches grew.

Wood

V shapes

Bark

Growth ring

TALLEST REDWOODS

The redwoods of California (*Sequoia sempervirens*), shown here, are the tallest trees in the world. The giant redwood (*Sequoiadendron giganteum*) is slightly shorter but it is the world's largest and heaviest tree.

Redwood
328 ft (100 m)

Norfolk pine
197 ft (60 m)

Balsam fir
82 ft (25 m)

Flowering Plants

Flowering plants are the most recent and the most dominant plants in the plant kingdom. There are more than a quarter of a million species of flowering plant, such as garden flowers, wildflowers, vegetables, grasses, trees and shrubs (with fruits not cones), vines and some water plants. Whether the flowers are large or small, beautiful or plain, they all contain the plant's reproductive structures or sex cells. The color and scent of some flowers attract birds or insects. The visitors feed mostly on the nectar or sugary water inside, then flit from flower to flower and carry the male pollen to the female stigma. Grasses and other plants with less obvious or attractive flowers rely on the wind to carry their pollen. Because the wind scatters the pollen, rather than taking it directly from flower to flower, these plants release millions of pollen grains. At least some of this pollen will reach the female stigma.

A STORM OF POLLEN
Grasses have small, unscented flowers arranged in spikelets at the end of the stem. In summer the wind scatters millions of grass pollen grains. They can cause hay fever, but without the pollen we would have no wheat, oats, barley, rice or corn to eat.

PERFECT PARTNERS
Birds are attracted to red flowers. The streamertail's small head and beak allow it to search for nectar in the pendant firebird's flower. The bird picks up pollen as it feeds.

LOOK AT ME!
Size, shape, scent and color attract insects to showy flowers. They also attract gardeners and botanists who try to improve on nature. Some of the flowers shown here are hybrids that can be produced naturally or artificially by cross-pollination.

NEW GENES

The male pumpkin flower (below), which withers and dies after it has released its pollen, grows on the same vine as the female flower (below). The male can pollinate a female sister flower and this is called self-pollination. The new plant is very similar to the parent plant, but cannot survive environmental changes as well as plants with genes from two separate parents. To avoid self-pollination, male and female flowers on the same plant often mature at different times. In some species, male and female flowers grow on separate plants and this ensures cross-pollination.

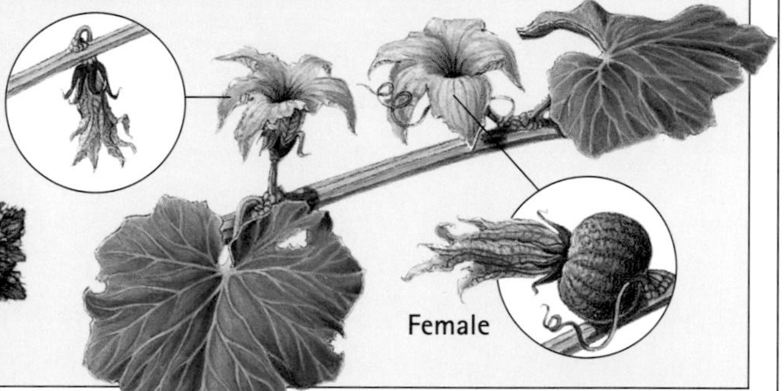

Male

Female

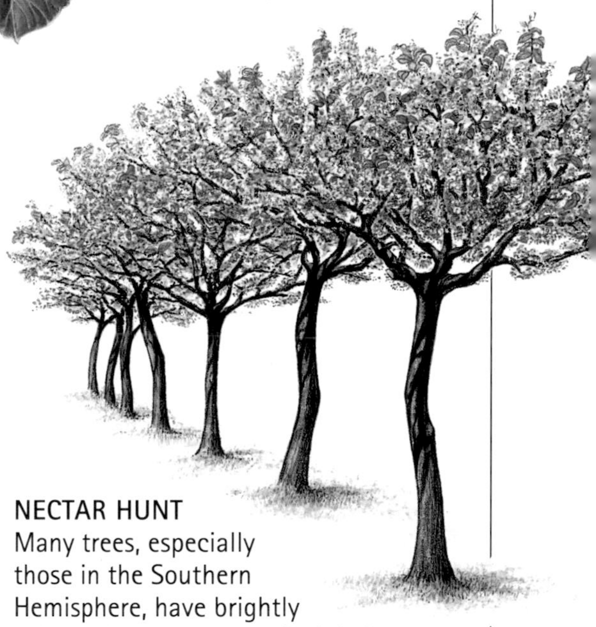

NECTAR HUNT

Many trees, especially those in the Southern Hemisphere, have brightly colored flowers. Insects find their way easily to the nectar at the center of the Judas tree flower. On the way to the nectar, they pick up or brush off pollen.

STRANGE BUT TRUE

The *Amorphophallus titanum* grows to a height of 12 ft (3.7 m) in the rainforests of Indonesia. The internal cluster of flowers opens for a few days and smells like rotten fish mixed with burnt sugar. Flies love the smell and come to lay their eggs. They also act as pollinators.

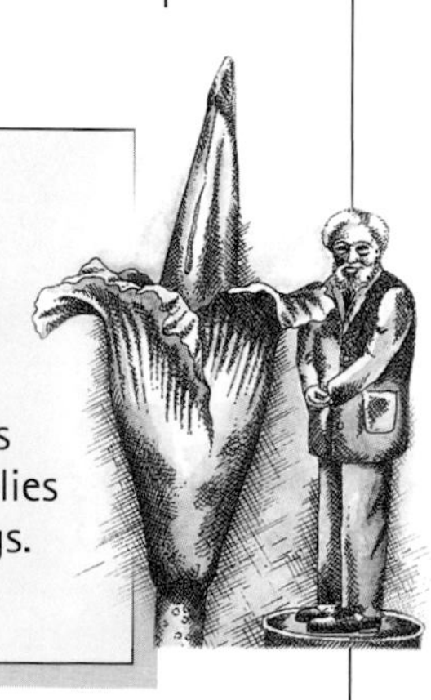

Discover more in New Life

25

The Life of Flowering Plants

Some flowering plants live, grow, disperse their seeds and die all within one spring and summer. These plants are called annuals. In spring an annual germinates from a seed, in summer it flowers and produces seeds inside a fruit, in autumn it withers and dies. But it does leave behind its seeds, which lie dormant over winter and germinate when spring arrives. Other flowering plants, including many trees, continue to live and grow year after year. These plants are called perennials. In temperate climates, where there are four seasons, perennials rest and stop growing in the cold of autumn and winter. Trees may drop their leaves during this rest period. Some plants, like the sweet potato (above left), survive the rest period on food stored in bulbs or stem tubers below the ground. Plants in tropical monsoon climates, where there is no autumn or winter, grow and reproduce when it is wet, but rest when it is dry.

A BRIEF BLOOM
During the few weeks of the very short Arctic summer, the sun never sets. With enough light, water from melting snow and some warmth, plants quickly flower and disperse their seeds before the cold, dark Arctic days return.

FOUR SEASONS
A London plane tree has four very different stages in its yearly cycle. This tree grows tall and strong, even in city streets, and is tough enough to resist pollution.

Spring
The numerous yellow male and red female flowers hang in separate, globular clusters on the same tree. Once fertilized, the female flower begins to grow fruit.

Summer
During summer, the clusters of tightly packed green fruits grow larger and protect the seeds inside.

26

WET AND DRY SEASONS

Temperate areas of the world have four seasons each year. Tropical monsoon areas have only two seasons—the wet season and the dry season. For plants growing in these areas, the wet season is the same as spring and summer when most of the growing takes place, the flowers bloom and the seeds disperse. In the dry season, the plants rest and some even drop their leaves to reduce the amount of water they lose. Just as plants in temperate regions have adapted to survive the cold winter months, these baobabs in Australia have adapted to survive the months when water is in short supply and fire is a constant danger.

FOOD STORES
The daffodil bulb stores food to use when it rests between growing and reproducing. Like an onion, the bulb is a series of concentric rings. These are the swollen bases of the leaves from the last season. In spring, new stems and leaves appear above the ground.

EVERGREEN COLOR
An evergreen grows new leaves before losing the old ones. In winter, when many other plants are leafless, the leaves and red berries of the holly provide a splash of color.

Autumn
As the leaves begin to change color, the hairy fruits also change from green to brown. They are dispersed by the wind.

Winter
The leaves and their stalks drop off the branches. The sticky buds on the end of the bare twigs protect the young leaves, which emerge in the spring.

Discover more in Forest Views

27

Plant Imposters

Fungi do not really belong in the plant kingdom. The 70,000 species of fungi, which include mushrooms, molds, mildews and rust on plants, have no roots, stems or leaves and no chlorophyll to make their own food. They feed on other plants and animals—dead or alive. Most fungi are made up of branching threadlike cells called hyphae, which break down living or dead cells into substances they can digest. They can digest almost anything, including the cellulose of plant cell walls. Their own cell walls are made of much stronger material, otherwise they might eat themselves. Fungi do not need light to produce food and often grow in the dark. Sometimes only the fruiting body appears above the surface in which the fungus is growing. When the fruiting body of a fungus releases its spores, the wind carries billions of them through the air.

COSTLY PARASITE
Rust is a parasitic fungus that can grow and feed on wheat. It damages the leaves, which produce sugars, and the wheat crop is much smaller or ruined.

A PUFF OF SPORES
Puffballs produce spores inside the hollow ball of the fungus. As the outside of the ball becomes hard and rigid, any knock causes the ball to vibrate and puff out spores.

LOOK BEFORE YOU EAT
Mushrooms are fungi that form fruiting bodies. Some of these are good to eat and others are deadly poisonous. But it is very difficult to tell which is which. Poisonous mushrooms, often called toadstools, can look more attractive than mushrooms that are safe to eat.

Underneath the cap
Spores form on gills underneath the cap. In just a few days, the spores shoot out of the gills and the fruiting body dies.

Stalk of threads
Hundreds of hyphae, compacted together, make up the column or stalk of the mushroom.

Thread network
The long threads of hyphae consume dead or decaying plant parts underground. The more they feed, the more they spread.

Ghost fungi

Cup fungi

Bracket fungi

Conical slimy cap

STRANGE BUT TRUE
This mushroom grows and glows on the forest floor of tropical rainforests. Scientists are not certain why the fungus glows in the dark. Perhaps the green light attracts nocturnal animals to help distribute the mushroom's spores.

SPACE INVADER
Parasites are fungi that feed and grow on live animals and plants. This fungus invaded the spider's body and slowly ate it.

Scarlet flycap

Parasol mushroom

MOLDY WONDER DRUG
If you leave bread, an apple or an orange in your schoolbag for a few days, a fungus, or mold, called penicillium may grow on it. You certainly would not want to eat the lunch once you found it but, in fact, penicillium saves millions of lives every year. Penicillin, an antibiotic extracted from penicillium (grown in a laboratory rather than in your schoolbag), cures many bacterial diseases. Penicillium also gives some cheeses their blue veins—and their strong taste and smell.

Forest fungi

Angel of death

SNIFFING FOR TREASURE
One of the world's most rare and expensive foods is a fungus. The fruiting part of a truffle grows underground and is sniffed out by pigs.

Aspen Bolete

Lady's veil

How Plants Survive

Plants, animals and humans cannot live and grow without water, minerals and food. They must also have some way of defending themselves from danger. Unlike animals and humans, however, plants cannot move around to find what they need, nor can they run from danger. Instead plants have evolved and adapted to their environment by growing special structures or developing unusual means for survival. Some plants have special roots or hairs to get the vital water they need from places other than the soil. Parasite plants have special roots that allow them to get all, or most of, their food and water from another plant. Carnivorous plants have special leaves or hairs to trap insects, which provide the plants with extra minerals. Many plants have prickers, thorns and poisons to protect themselves from sucking insects, pecking birds or chomping animals.

THE WORLD'S LARGEST FLOWER
Rafflesia, a parasite, spends most of its life living inside a rainforest vine. For a short time, it breaks through the stem, flowers and attracts flies as pollinators. Then it dies.

CLOSE TO THE LIGHT
Tropical orchids can germinate and spend all their lives high in trees. They produce their own food and absorb water from the damp air through special dangling aerial roots.

DID YOU KNOW?

The deadly nightshade plant produces a poison called atropine. Women in Renaissance Europe dropped atropine into their eyes to enlarge the pupils and make them look more beautiful. That is why the plant has another name, belladonna, which means "beautiful lady" in Italian. Atropine from belladonna is still used in eye surgery today.

POISONOUS PROTECTION

Many plants produce poisons in their leaves, flowers, sap, fruits or seed coats. Buttercup flowers, castor-oil beans and the sap of some canes are all poisonous. Uncooked cashew nuts have a poison that blisters the mouth. Often one part of the plant may be poisonous to deter predators while other parts are harmless to attract potential pollinators. Insects avoid the poisonous leaves of some tomato plants, but other animals eat the fruits of tomato plants and disperse their seeds.

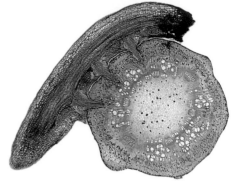

SUCKING ROOTS
Parasites have special roots that attach to and pierce the roots or stem of the host plant. The parasite then absorbs sugar, water and mineral salts directly from the host.

Sweet smells
The color of the pitcher and the smell of nectar attracts an unsuspecting insect to the lid.

A closer look
To reach the nectar the insect has to leave the safety of the lid and land on the slippery mouth of the pitcher.

False flower
The pitcher looks like a beautiful flower but it is really a large leaf tip.

A BARBED WARNING
Roses have thorns, or barbed growths, attached to their stems. The thorns snag painfully on animals that get too close and warn them to keep away.

Tumbling down
Losing its foothold, the insect falls into the pitcher. Special downward-pointing hairs keep it from climbing or flying back up.

Trapped
The insect drowns in the pool of digestive juices at the bottom. The plant absorbs the minerals from the insect leaving only its shell.

MINERAL SUPPLEMENTS
Pitcher plants grow in wet, boggy soil that does not provide all the minerals they need. To get extra minerals, they trap and digest insects, such as wasps.

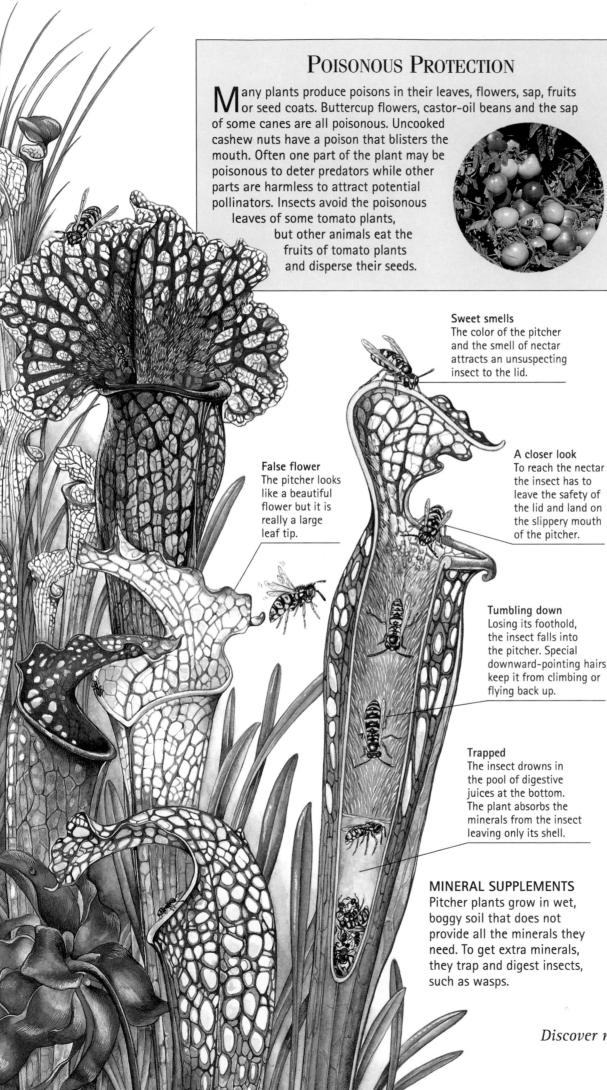

DEW TRAP
Hairs on the sundew's leaves produce a sticky, digestive liquid. Insects think it is water, but stick fast when they land. The liquid then digests them.

Discover more in Germination and Growth

COLOR BLAZE
A mixed forest in autumn is ablaze with the green leaves of evergreen trees and the brown, yellow, orange and red leaves of deciduous trees.

SPRING FLOWERS
Decaying leaves from trees add nutrients to the soil. In spring, before new leaves have grown on the trees, there is plenty of light for flowers to grow.

Forest Views

Forests in Canada or Russia are different from the forests in France, India, Indonesia or Australia. Climate and soil influence the kind of trees that grow in a forest, and the trees determine what grows on the forest floor beneath them. In cold, northern latitudes, evergreen conifers grow in boreal forests (named after Boreas, the Greek god of the north wind), but few plants grow on these dark forest floors. In temperate regions of the world, spring flowers grow on the floor of deciduous forests, where the trees shed their leaves in winter. Mixed forests of different kinds of conifers and flowering trees grow in some parts of the world. In tropical rainforests, growth occurs almost throughout the year, but in tropical monsoon forests, where there is a wet and a dry season, trees and plants on the forest floor grow mainly in the wet season. In the eucalypt forests of Australia, a variety of vegetation grows on the forest floor.

BANDS OF FOREST
Regions on the same latitude, above or below the equator, tend to have similar climates. This is why most types of forests grow in bands running east to west across many countries.

Boreal forests: northern parts of North America, Europe and Russia

Deciduous forests: eastern USA, most of Europe, eastern China and Japan

Mixed forests: western USA, southern Chile and parts of Argentina and New Zealand

Tropical rainforests: South America, Central Africa, Southeast Asia and northeast Australia

Tropical monsoon forests: South America, India, northern Australia and parts of Southeast Asia and Africa

Eucalypt forests: Australia

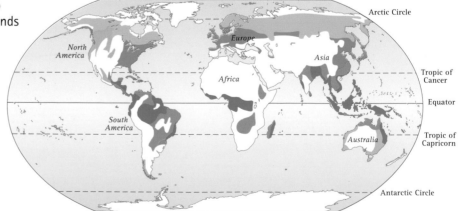

Rainforest Floor

GOOD MATCH
This passion vine plant, which climbs up from the forest floor, produces an organic poison to deter leaf-eating insects. But this butterfly is immune to the passion vine's poison and is able to lay its eggs on the plant. It also acts as a pollinator.

The rainforest floor is cool, damp and dark. The few plants that grow there have adapted to low light. They usually have extra-large leaves to capture what little light there is. They grow slowly and can flower, often brilliantly, without much sunlight. But the most common plants of the forest floor are the seedlings, or saplings, of tall canopy trees. These small saplings are "trees of the future"—waiting for the death of a tall canopy tree. When a tree falls, light appears through the space it filled in the canopy and the race is on among the saplings to be the first to fill the space and grow rapidly. Rainforest soils are low in nutrients. The floor is covered by a layer of dead animal and plant material, much of which falls from the canopy. Fungi, bacteria and insects break down this material and release nutrients into the soil. However, instead of remaining in the soil, most of the nutrients are quickly absorbed by the roots of plants.

DID YOU KNOW?
The major digesters of plant materials on the rainforest floor are fungi and millions of invisible bacteria. If they did not decompose and recycle the nutrients from plants, the rainforest floor would be buried under a mountain of plant waste.

KEEPING OUT THE COLD
The needle shape and waxy outer coating of conifer leaves allow them to tolerate the cold and shrug off snow. Evergreen conifers allow little light to reach the forest floor. Dwarf evergreen shrubs, mosses and lichens are all that you will see there.

NEW LIFE
A forest fire burns the leaves of tall trees and clears the undergrowth. Dormant seeds now have enough light and space to germinate in soil that is rich in nutrients from the ash.

EUCALYPT FORESTS

The Australian continent drifted and became separated from the rest of the world around 50 million years ago. With no competition from species that dominated other parts of the world, unusual animals and plants were able to flourish in Australia. The dominant trees are the 500 species of eucalypt or gum tree that grow in forests in both temperate and tropical regions of Australia. Like conifers they are evergreens but their leaves hang down and allow light to reach the forest floor.

Discover more in Plant Industries

Tropical Rainforests

A tropical rainforest is home to a wider range of plants and animals than any other habitat. In these steamy, teeming jungles, the air is always warm and humid. When it rains, it rains hard. Many leaves have a special drip tip, as shown above, to funnel away excess water that might "drown" the leaf cells and stomata. High above the ground, the leaves of tall trees almost meet to form a roof, or canopy, of green. Some trees, called emergents, grow as tall as 20-storey buildings and rise above the canopy, which lets only a little light through. To get their share of the light, many plants, called epiphytes, seed, germinate and grow on the trunk or branches of tall trees. Vines and lianas (the thick, woody-stemmed vines that Tarzan used for swinging through the forest) use tall trees like scaffolding. They climb, cling or coil upwards to the light. Some plants start from a seed high in a tree and grow downwards to take root in the soil.

STRANGLER FIG

This epiphyte grows from a bird-borne seed high in the host tree. It grows roots down into the soil and forms a woody "corset" around the trunk. Because the tree cannot grow outwards, it dies and rots away. The strangler fig now stands alone.

Woody "corset" of the strangler fig

A CHANGING CANOPY

When the trees that form the canopy are damaged or die, they become trees of the past. Trees of the future—saplings or partly grown trees—begin to grow in their place.

A CANOPY VIEW

This is the view that many animals have of the rainforest. Plants in the canopy get water from the atmosphere and rain, and nutrients from airborne debris. They use sunlight for photosynthesis. Animals eat nectar, fruits, seeds and leaves.

DEAD OR ALIVE?
This tree may be dead but it is alive with activity. Mosses, seedlings and ferns grow on it. Animals move in and feed on the bark and wood, seeds and leaves around it. Fungi and bacteria break down and recycle the phosphorous, nitrogen and other nutrients. The log will soon disappear but new plants will fill the space.

Decomposers
Networks of hyphae from many different fungi grow rapidly. They break down and absorb the dead cells on the log.

New plants
A gap in the canopy gives a few saplings the light they need to grow.

Spot the moth
Difficult to spot among the leaf litter, this moth grew from a caterpillar, the most common leafeater of the rainforest.

Life in
the Desert

Lack of water and intense daytime heat are the main problems for plants that grow in the desert. The roots of most desert plants go deep or spread out widely in search of every drop of water. Rain may fall in the desert only once every few years, so storing this precious water is vital. Plants store water in swollen roots, in succulent (juicy) leaves or in stems with ridges that can expand to hold it. But water is still lost, mainly through the leaves and other green parts. Some plants drop their leaves or grow spines instead of leaves. Many desert plants have a waxy coating on their leaves with stomata buried in pits rather than on the surface of the leaf. Succulent plants have a special photosynthesis system that can operate without the stomata being open in dry periods. But some plants avoid these problems altogether. They spend most of their lives as dormant seeds and complete their very short life cycle only when rainfall is good.

A BRILLIANT BURST
Desert annuals grow, flower, fruit and disperse their seeds in a few short weeks after rain. Their seeds often have a chemical coating that prevents germination, sometimes for many years. Only a really good shower of rain washes this coating away. When it does, the desert blooms.

A SLOW LIFE
The saguaro grows very slowly. Branches begin to grow from quite high up the stem when the plant is "middle-aged."

Years 10   50   75   100   150-200

IN THE MIDDAY SUN
The tall green stem of the giant saguaro cactus makes the plant's food supply. The stomata are closed to cut down water loss. The saguaro cactus provides a home for woodpeckers while a ground-squirrel gets water from the beaver-tail cactus.

Sunblocking spines
The tufted spines on the chain-fruit cholla reflect and scatter the fierce rays of the sun.

40

EAT AND BE EATEN

Most snails are plant eaters that absorb the nutrients manufactured by plants. Snails then provide meals, and processed nutrients, for meat eaters.

ENERGY FLOW

Dead plant and animal remains are the raw materials for the rainforest nutrient cycle. The dead cells must be broken down by fungi and bacteria before the nutrients can be released into the soil. Fungi can also grow on or into tree roots, helping them absorb the nutrients.

Consumers

Termites eat, or consume, large quantities of plant litter, especially bark and wood. Their mounds, full of rich nutrients, are absorbed by the poor soil.

Plant growth

Most plants grow at their tips. The cells here are sm... and numerous. Activity inside the cells chan... along the grow... tip as shown.

Young leaves

Cells divide and increase in number

Cells increase in size

Cells develop into xylem, phloem or chloroplast cells

Living animals

Droppings and dead animals

Bacteria

Dead plants

Fungi

Living plants

Nutrients released into soil

RECYCLED INGREDIENTS

Like all epiphytes growing on host trees high in the rainforest, the tank bromeliad produces food in its leaves. But the tough leaves are also shaped to collect up to 2 gallons (10 liters) of water. The water attracts a large assortment of insects, reptiles, birds and animals, which deposit droppings. The droppings, together with leaves and airborne dust, gather in a nutrient-rich "soup" in the plant. This is absorbed by the bromeliad and used to help produce its food.

GIVE AND TAKE
Ants live inside the cavities of the epiphytic ant plant. They bring dead insects to the plant and produce droppings. These decay and give the plant mineral nutrients to use in photosynthesis.

Inside the cavities

FRUITS OF THE FOREST
Animals have a rich selection of fruits to eat. They swallow some fruits whole and pass the seeds out in droppings. They eat the fleshy fruit of others and spit out the seeds.

Discover more in Plant Processes

SHALLOW ROOTS

In temperate forests the roots of trees grow deep into the soil where the nutrients lie (bottom left). As the soil in tropical rainforests is not rich in nutrients, the trees here have shallow roots near or on the surface of the soil. These trap surface water as well as leaves and other waste. The nutrients released when the waste decomposes are quickly absorbed by the roots. Some rainforest tree trunks have large finlike growths at the base called buttresses. They compensate for the shallow roots and can extend 30 ft (10 m) up the trunk to support the tree's weight.

Shallow roots near the surface

Leafcutter ants
The ants snip off pieces of leaf. Back in the nest, they chew the pieces into "compost" on which their real food—a fungus—grows.

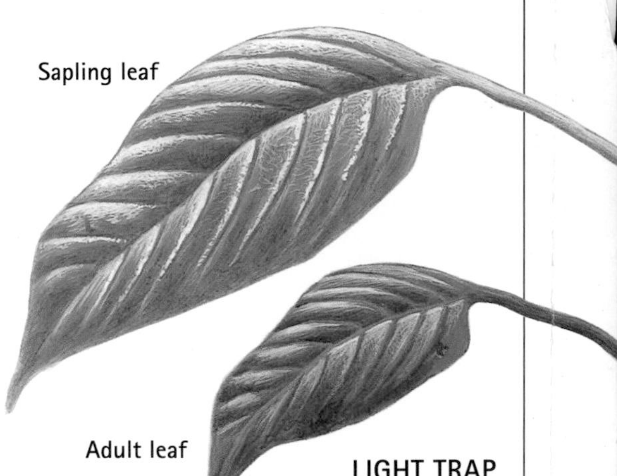

Sapling leaf

Adult leaf

LIGHT TRAP
The many small leaves of the adult rainforest tree catch the light. A sapling has fewer leaves but they are bigger to absorb what little light hits the forest floor.

Discover more in Plant Imposters

NEVER-ENDING LEAVES

The bizarre welwitschia, a distant cone-bearing relative of the conifers, grows in the drought-ridden Namib Desert of Africa. Two leaves grow like long straps from the flat cushion of the stem and continue growing throughout the plant's very long life. Wind, and the sand it stirs up, may tatter the leaves of the welwitschia, which in a 2,000-year-old plant may be 26 ft (8 m) long. The leaves trap moisture from the early morning dew and fog, and channel it down to the swollen tap root.

WATER SEARCH

The mesquite tree (above left) sends its roots down deep to tap into the water table far below. The cactus (above right) sends its roots out horizontally in search of every drop of surface water.

LIVING STONES

The two round, fat leaves of the stone plant look like stones, because stones do not attract grazing animals. Most of the plant remains underground, hidden from the fierce sun.

IN THE COOL OF THE NIGHT

As the sun sets, the stomata in the cacti open to balance the gases in the plants that are generated by their special photosynthesis system. A nocturnal bat goes from flower to flower and is the saguaro's main pollinator.

Facing away

The flat pads of beaver-tail cacti face the warmth of the late afternoon and early morning sun. When the sun is high, they face sideways to avoid the intense heat.

SURVIVAL TECHNIQUES

The succulent leaves and the soft fiber inside the trunk of the quiver tree store water. The white-powdered branches and pale trunk reflect the sun's rays and stop the tree from overheating.

Grasslands

Grasslands occur in areas that get more rain than deserts but not as much rain as forests. They have few trees, and some have no trees at all. Grasses are hardier than trees and lose less water in dry winds than taller plants. The horizontal stems of some grasses prevent wet areas from eroding. As a weapon against competitors, many grasses secrete a chemical that reduces the nutrients available for other plants. Grasses are enormously varied. Some grow in tussocks and others grow in mats (like lawns). Some are perennials and others are annuals. Many grow only to knee height but some, like sugar cane, grow tall. Grasses are flowering plants that reproduce sexually. Many can also reproduce from horizontal stems above the ground (stolons) or just below the ground (rhizomes). These stems are often hollow with solid joints or nodes from which new grass plants sometimes sprout.

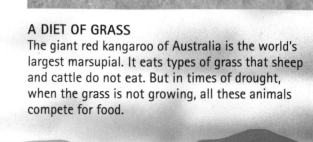

A DIET OF GRASS
The giant red kangaroo of Australia is the world's largest marsupial. It eats types of grass that sheep and cattle do not eat. But in times of drought, when the grass is not growing, all these animals compete for food.

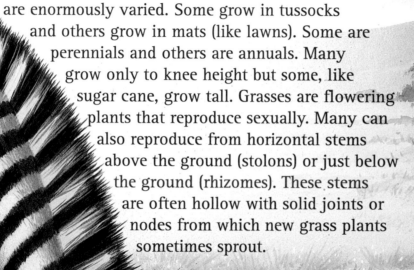

AFRICAN SAVANNA
Savanna animals graze on different types and ages of grass. Grass continues to grow when the upper part of the leaf is eaten because the growing cells are at the base of the grass leaf rather than the tip.

THE GRASSHOUSE BUILDER

Large animals of the grasslands have no place to hide. They rely on speed rather than hiding places to escape danger. But for many birds the grasslands are a safe haven with plenty of building material. Weaver birds use grass to weave complex nests on the ground or in one of the few trees (above). One tree may hold as many as 400 nests. The social weaver bird, however, builds one huge nest with a roof of grass and sticks. This nest has a separate chamber for each pair of birds that live there.

DID YOU KNOW?

A female elephant who has just given birth eats 440 lb (200 kg) of grass, leaves and fruits a day. She bulldozes and uproots trees to get her rations.

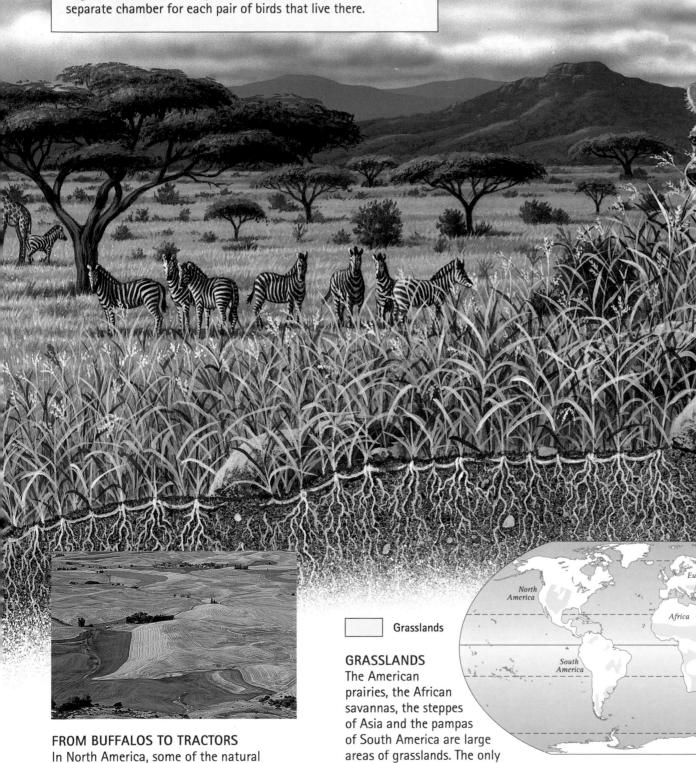

FROM BUFFALOS TO TRACTORS
In North America, some of the natural grasslands where buffalo once fed are now planted with wheat, a grass food crop.

Grasslands

GRASSLANDS
The American prairies, the African savannas, the steppes of Asia and the pampas of South America are large areas of grasslands. The only continent that does not have grassland is Antarctica.

North America

Europe

Asia

Africa

South America

Australia

Discover more in Flowering Plants

43

AN ALPINE FLOWER
Edelweiss grows in cracks in rocks. Its waxy leaves reduce water loss and its leaf hairs help to prevent heat loss. The large flowers attract pollinating insects when they flower briefly.

• WHERE PLANTS LIVE •
Extreme Lives

It is difficult for plants to live in the cold temperatures, chilling winds and low rainfall of the polar regions and high mountain tops. In Antarctica, only one flowering plant (a grass), and lichens, mosses and algae can survive the severe conditions. But in the Arctic tundra, and on high mountains around the world, some plants have adapted to the extreme conditions. As you climb higher or travel nearer to the North Pole, the temperature drops. Stands of conifers give way to occasional, stunted, ground-hugging tree species until you reach an area known as the tree line. Beyond this, life is impossible for trees. For the low-growing plants above or beyond the tree line, the growing season is short. As rainfall is low, many have waxy leaves to cut down water loss. Many also have hairy stems and leaves to prevent the loss of water and heat. The hairs also protect the plant from damaging ultraviolet rays, which are stronger at high altitudes than in any other environment. Some plants even have special cell sap to prevent the plant's cells from freezing solid.

THAWING OUT
In the Arctic tundra, the soil is permanently frozen. When snow and ice melt, the water cannot penetrate the frozen soil, so it gathers on top. Some plants have adapted to this stagnant water.

44

STRANGE BUT TRUE

The Arctic buttercup's white flower and shape reflect and focus the sun's rays into the center of the flower. This little pool of heat attracts insect pollinators. After pollination, the flower darkens to reduce reflection and absorbs the warmth for the growing ovary.

GIANT OF THE ANDES

This giant woody-stemmed herb, the puya, lives for up to 150 years. The prickly rosette folds upwards around the stem to keep the plant warm during the cold mountain nights.

ODD-SHAPED STRAGGLERS

Between the last of the tall straight trees and the low-growing plants beyond the tree line, a few straggling trees survive. They are often stunted dwarves, twisted into strange shapes by fierce winds. The branches of some grow only on the side of the tree that is away from chilling winds and blasting snow. Some tree species grow along the ground instead of up from it. They reach only a few inches in height but their stretched-out length can equal the height of a medium-sized lowland relative.

HUDDLED TOGETHER

This cushion plant in the mountains of Tasmania, Australia, is not one, but many plants. Huddling tightly together creates a warmer and more humid environment, and the hard cushion of leaves keeps out the worst of the cold, drying wind.

ARCTIC TUNDRA

At the tree line, the trees are bare on the windblown side. Low-growing flowering plants, grasses, mosses and lichens survive better near ground level, where the temperature is warmer and the wind less chilling. In summer there is water and warmth for a short growing season.

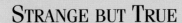

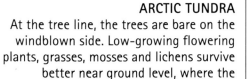

By the Sea

There are many different coastal environments, and different plants, where the land meets the sea. If you stand at the high-tide mark on a sandy beach and look towards the sea, you will notice that plants do not grow on the wet sand between high and low tide. The waves would soon uproot any plants that grew there. However, on rocks exposed between high and low tide, you will see algae growing. If you turn and look towards the land, you are looking at grasses—the "front line" of the land-plant community. Their long underground stems and strong tufts bind the sand and stop it from blowing away in the wind. Behind the grasses, the dunes become more stable as the roots of salt-resistant and wind-resistant plants take a firm hold. Beyond these low-growing plants, forests of trees grow in the sandy soil. In estuaries, where land and river meet the sea, there is no clearly defined beach. Tropical mangroves or temperate salt marshes thrive here.

SURVIVING STILL
On exposed rocks or rock platforms, lichens keep on growing, slowly, year after year. These hardy survivors can cope with being splashed by the coldest of seas and salt spray.

WHERE RIVER MEETS SEA
Grasses and shrubs bind the sediments brought down by the river to the estuary. Many salt marsh plants have succulent leaves, which store fresh water.

WINDBLOWN SAND
On an Australian beach, hardy plants resistant to salt spray help to stabilize shifting sands. The plants closest to the water trap the sand, and the taller canopies in the dunes reduce the wind.

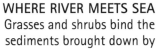

SAILING FRUIT
The sea and the wind transport the buoyant fruit of the screw-pine to islands or coastal land great distances away from the parent plant.

Foredunes
Animals eat the fruits of coastal pigface, a creeping herb. Its stems run along or just below the semi-stable sand.

Above the sea
Blue-green algae, which are almost black, cling to rocks that are splashed by waves.

Splash zone

Between high and low tide
On rocks that are underwater at high tide but exposed to the air at low tide, you will see brown, ribbonlike wracks and bright green seaweeds.

Intertidal zone

Below the sea
Here you will see the red seaweeds or huge brown kelps that spend most of their lives covered by the sea and become exposed only if the tide is very low.

COLOR ZONES
On rocky shorelines, at low tide, you can see different types of colored algae. Each has a particular preference for one zone of the sea. Tidepools contain the greatest number of species in one place.

Subtidal zone

FROM BARE SAND TO FOREST

The seeds of grasses and herbs, carried by the wind or birds, germinate in the bare sand of a coral island. As their roots bind the sand, low-growing plants and a ring of shrubs begin to grow in the more stable sand behind them and away from the sea. Within this protective ring, trees take root and what was once bare sand becomes green forest. But if seas wash over the island or animals trample the plants, the island will return to an earlier stage of plant development or become bare sand once again.

High canopy
The canopy of the coastal banksia trees deflects and reduces the strong sea breezes.

High dunes
Coastal wattle grows along the ground, acting as wind and sand barriers.

Close to the sea
Beach spinifex is an efficient sand binder. The female fruiting head cartwheels on its spines along the sand, dispersing seeds as it goes.

SALT WATER
Mangroves cope with high salt levels by excreting excess salt through special leaf cells or by sending the salt to dying leaves, which then drop off.

Freshwater Worlds

Many different freshwater plants grow in the running water of streams and rivers or the still, calmer waters of ponds and lakes. They live at various depths, as long as the light they need for photosynthesis can reach them. Some freshwater plants float freely on top of the water, with hairlike roots that do not anchor the plant but do absorb nutrients from the water. Others spend their lives submerged underwater. Free-floating and submerged plants usually have soft green stems. Spaces between their cells are filled with water and gas. These hold them up towards the light as effectively as stiff stems. Emergent, or "wet-feet", plants however, have stiff stems, which hold part of the plant above the water while the roots and lower part remain under water. Nearly all water plants can flower and reproduce sexually. Most have inconspicuous flowers and rely on wind or water to pollinate. Life is not always easy for water plants. Their environment is prone to disturbances such as changing water levels and pollution.

A FREE-FLOATING TAKEOVER
The water hyacinth, a native of Central America, has been introduced to many waterways around the world. It is carried by wind and water, and spreads rapidly, often becoming a pest. It can push other plants out and take over the waterway.

FOOD CHAIN
Microscopic plants, called phytoplankton (left), provide food for small crustaceans and insects, called zooplankton. When a carnivorous fish eats the zooplankton it gets some of the plant's energy. The fish's waste provides nutrients for other plants.

Duckweed
The smallest of flowering plants, this is a favorite snack for ducks. Hairlike roots balance the plant and draw nutrients from the water.

Water nymph
You cannot see the water nymph, which flowers underwater, but you can see its bubbles of oxygen at the water's surface during photosynthesis.

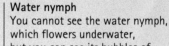

HOLDING ON
The fast-flowing water in rivers can uproot plants and rip leaves to shreds. This tropical plant can survive in such waters because it has strong holdfasts and its fine leaves last only a few weeks. The short, thick leaf bases then continue the plant's photosynthesis.

Bulrushes
This emergent plant is closely related to grasses. Its flowers are small and its stiff stem holds it above the water.

Weeping willow
The willow can tolerate soggy soil. The leaves that it sheds add nutrients to the mud in the pond.

Water milfoil
The leaves under the water help to balance the plant. The broad leaves above the water collect light.

Algae
On stones, in or above the water, slimy algae take hold.

Water lily
The lily's soft stems carry oxygen from the air down to the roots. The flower attracts insect pollinators.

LIFE IN A VILLAGE POND
Plants on the bank, in the shallows, or in deep but sunlit water provide food and shelter for many animals. Plant and animal waste ends up at the bottom of the pond, where scavengers and fungi break it down into usable nutrients.

FROM WATER TO WETLAND

Over thousands of years, lakes can change into wetland, an environment halfway between land and water. Rivers running into the lake deposit sediment, or silt. The lake bed rises and the water depth drops. Land plants take root on the silt at the shoreline. Water plants move towards the center of the lake. More silt and plant debris build up. Peat forms under the marsh, on which more land plants and water-tolerant trees take root. What was a habitat for water plants is now wetland, dominated by land plants.

Lake

Marsh

Swamp or wetland

PLANT CROPS
On one-fifth of the world's cultivated land, fully mechanized farms produce 539 million tons (550 million tonnes) of wheat each year. We eat most of it, but one-fifth is used to feed farm animals.

SPOONFULS OF SUGAR
More than half of the world's sugar comes from the thick, jointed stems of sugar cane, which is a tropical grass. The cane is cut just above ground level, leaving the stem to sprout new shoots for next year's crop.

PLANT PROTEIN
Nuts are rich in protein and fats. They provided a nutritious alternative to meat in the Stone Age and are now eaten by vegetarians for the same reason. Hundreds of species of trees and shrubs produce nuts, but not all of them are true nuts and only 20–30 species are cultivated on nut farms.

• PLANTS AND HUMANS •

Food Plants

The first humans were nomads. They were constantly on the move, gathering wild plants and hunting wild animals for food. Some nomads realized that if they cultivated plants, as food for themselves and for the animals they herded, they could remain settled in one place. Since they had no form of transportation—apart from feet—the fruits, vegetables and grasses or grains they cultivated were those that grew wild within walking distance. Wild wheat and barley crops were grown in the Middle East, rice was cultivated in China and wild maize (Indian corn) in Central and South America. As trade around the world increased during the sixteenth century, plant crops became trade goods that were taken from one part of the world to another. With growing populations to feed, farmers began to grow greater quantities of crops to feed themselves and to sell to others. Today, wherever you live in the world, you can eat grains, fruits, vegetables and nuts whose plant ancestors grew wild in another far corner of the world.

TEA LEAVES

When tea was introduced to the rest of the world from China, it was considered an exotic, fashionable drink. Today, it is drunk by many people. Only the young leaf tips are picked, then fermented, dried and crushed.

WILD FOODS

Most of the food we eat today has been grown on farms, but food plants still grow in the wild, just as they did in Stone Age times. Fruits, berries, leaves and nuts can be picked. Tubers, bulbs and roots can be dug up and eaten.

TERRACES OF RICE

For more than 5,000 years, rice has been planted in China and Southeast Asia in water-filled paddy fields or terraces cut into the hillside. Rice is the main grain of more than half the world's population.

FRUITS AND VEGETABLES

A fruit is the seed-bearing part of a plant; other edible parts are vegetables.

 A strawberry is a fruit with many ovaries, each with a single seed.

 An orange is the fruit of an evergreen tree.

 A carrot is an orange-colored tap root.

 A potato is the thickened end of an underground stem, or rhizome, called a tuber.

 A tomato is a fruit originally from the Americas.

 An onion is an underground bulb that stores the plant's sugars.

 A pumpkin is a fruit grown on a vine. The seeds are also eaten.

 Ginger is an underground stem, or rhizome.

 A lettuce is a bunch of leaves, usually eaten raw.

 Asparagus is a green stem with reduced leaves, or bracts.

Discover more in Introducing Plants

ANCIENT REMEDY
Science has now proved what ancient people believed. The bulbs, or cloves, of garlic can help to cure bronchitis and colds as well as lowering cholesterol levels and blood pressure.

Medicines from Plants

Plants have always been a major source of medicines. By trial and error, early humans discovered that many plants could cure diseases, heal wounds or reduce pain. Among the early herbalists were some pioneers of medicine and pharmacology who studied the effects of certain plants on their patients. They recorded their discoveries in books called "herbals" so that their knowledge could be shared with others. This knowledge is still used by pharmaceutical companies to develop drugs that contain plant ingredients or synthetic substitutes. Traditional plant medicines can now be investigated and analyzed in laboratories. The questions that herbalists of previous times could not answer can now be answered. What is the main chemical ingredient of the plant part being used? How does it work on the human body? And, most importantly, what is the correct dosage that will cure the disease without killing the patient?

A MEASURED AMOUNT
In the Middle Ages, apothecaries were the equivalent of today's drug stores or pharmacies. Their medicines were mainly dried plants or herbs, not pills. The dosage was measured out very precisely, but people were still unsure how much it took to cure, or kill.

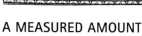

REGULAR HEARTBEAT
Foxglove leaves contain digitalin, a drug that keeps millions of heart patients alive today. There is no manufactured substitute for digitalin, which is powdered and used to regulate heartbeat.

TRADITIONAL CURE
In many parts of Asia, shops sell prepared herbal syrups and dried herbs, which the patient mixes in water before drinking. Many of these herbal remedies have been used for centuries.

DID YOU KNOW?
Ipecacuanha, which comes from the rhizomes and roots of a Brazilian native plant, is used in traditional villages and in modern homes. If someone accidentally swallows something poisonous, ipecac syrup makes them vomit and get rid of the poison.

CHEMICAL DETECTIVE WORK

For centuries, herbal medicines made from willow bark reduced fever and eased the pain and inflammation of aching joints and muscles. Although nineteenth-century chemists extracted the active element, called salicin, from the bark, it had unpleasant side effects such as nausea and ringing in the ears. In 1899, a chemist who was anxious to find a drug that would help his father's rheumatoid arthritis made a substance similar to salicin, but with fewer side effects. The drug, one of the most commonly used today, is known as aspirin.

PLANT GUM
Australian Aborigines use the red gum, or kino, from the bloodwood tree as a skin ointment. The kino helps to heal wounds, sores and rashes. Mixed with water and gargled, it also helps to cure a sore throat.

HERBAL MEDICINE
A village doctor in Asia grinds seeds to make herbal medicine. In many countries, especially those where doctors and hospitals are not available to everyone, some medicines are still made from plants. Scientists analyze their healing properties and develop synthetic substitutes.

ADDICTIVE PAINKILLER
A cut seed pod from an unripe opium poppy leaks a milky sap. The dried sap is opium, which contains the powerful painkillers morphine and codeine.

53

SAILING SHIPS
The forests of western Europe were plundered in the 1500s when galleons were built from hardwoods such as oak. The cleared forests became farming or grazing lands.

CORK STRIPS
Cork comes from the dead outer bark of the cork oak tree. The live inner bark grows a new layer of cork bark, which can be stripped again in eight to ten years.

A MANAGED FOREST
About one-quarter of the world's forests are not natural forests. Conifers, which grow rapidly, are planted in managed forests. As trees in one section are felled, seedlings are planted in other sections so the forest is constantly renewed.

Plant Industries

Many domestic items that we use every day come from the raw materials of plants. Sisal rope, as shown above, is made from a large herb. In earlier times, when populations were small and needs were simple, people built shelters from plant materials. They gathered plant fibers, which they spun and made into clothing. They made wooden bows and axe handles, and wove rope from the stems of flax plants. They gathered their own fuels, such as wood, coal and peat. All this changed during the Industrial Revolution when the first factories, growing urban populations and the development of transportation increased the demand for wood, coal, cotton, rubber and other plant materials. Large numbers of people harvested and processed these materials and new plant industries were born. By the 1800s, the forests in the industrialized countries of Europe were almost gone. Plant industries must be managed carefully today to ensure they do not destroy the plant resources of tomorrow.

Second thinning
After 20-30 years, more of the trees are removed.

Planting
Seedlings are planted close together so branches remain small and most of the growth is in the trunk.

Clear felling
The tree trunks are removed, but the branches and pine needles are left on the ground.

PULPED WOOD
Almost 40 per cent of the timber cut each year ends up in pulp mills. Here the bark is stripped off and the wood is ground into small chips that are chemically "cooked," dried and pressed into sheets. From these sheets, paper mills manufacture paper and cardboard.

NO WASTE
In some sawmills, computers are used to determine the maximum amount of usable wood. They generate a cutting pattern and program the mechanized saws for cutting.

NATURAL PLANT FIBERS
For centuries, people have worn clothes made of cotton and linen, which are natural plant fibers. Cotton comes from the white fibers that surround the seeds of the cotton plant (shown here). After the seed capsules are picked, the seeds and husks are removed, the longer fibers are spun into yarn and the shorter fibers are used for cotton wool. Linen, one of the strongest natural fibers, comes from the stem of the flax plant, which is soaked until partly decomposed. The fibers are then rolled or scraped off.

Ready for planting
A chopper roller mulches plant material into the ground before it is plowed.

First thinning
After 10–15 years, some trees are removed and used for fence posts or pulpwood.

Mature trees
The remaining trees reach maturity in 50-60 years.

STRANGE BUT TRUE
The Mayans of South America made their own shoes by dipping their feet into bowls of white sap from the trunks of rubber trees. They sat with their feet up for a few hours until the sap dried into soft, rubber shoes that were a perfect fit.

Discover more in Conifers and Their Relatives

Helping Nature

Food and textile plants today are the result of thousands of years of experimentation and research. Many of their original wild ancestors are now extinct. In their place we have cultivated plants that give higher yields or produce two crops each year, have better quality seeds or fruits, and are more able to resist disease or pests. The New Stone Age farmers started this process by selecting and planting seeds from the strongest and healthiest plants for the next year's crop. With the aid of the modern science of genetics, scientists can now cross-fertilize plants. The resulting plant often has the best features of each parent and is a genetic improvement on both. In another technique, called cloning, large numbers of identical plants can be produced from a small amount of plant tissue, even from a single cell of an adult plant. The technique of grafting, a form of vegetative propagation where part of one plant is attached to and grows on another closely related plant, has been used for 2,000 years.

MADE IN A TEST TUBE
A cutting from an adult plant, placed in a test tube containing a gel with growth hormones, will grow into a new plant called a clone. The clone is identical in size, shape and quality to the original plant.

Savoy cabbage
One very large bud grows at the end of the stem.

Broccoli
Many flower clusters grow at the top of the stem.

HUMAN CONTROLS
Inside a greenhouse, out-of-season fruits and vegetables, or plants that would normally grow only in warmer countries, thrive. The hours of light can also be altered to increase photosynthetic activity. This often speeds up the plants' growth and the development of flowers and fruits.

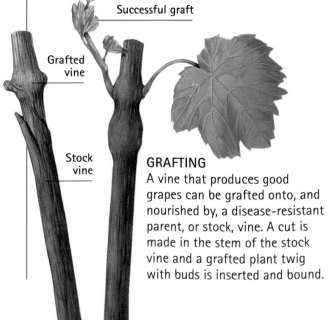

Successful graft

Grafted vine

Stock vine

GRAFTING
A vine that produces good grapes can be grafted onto, and nourished by, a disease-resistant parent, or stock, vine. A cut is made in the stem of the stock vine and a grafted plant twig with buds is inserted and bound.

Brussels sprouts
An enormous number of buds or sprouts grow from the sides of the stem.

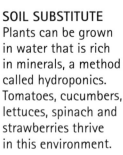

SOIL SUBSTITUTE
Plants can be grown in water that is rich in minerals, a method called hydroponics. Tomatoes, cucumbers, lettuces, spinach and strawberries thrive in this environment.

STRONG OFFSPRING

Many of the fruits, vegetables and grain we eat are hybrids. They are created by cross-fertilizing two related, purebred parents. Hybrids are more resistant to diseases and pests and produce more food for us than self-pollinating plants, which produce weak offspring after a few generations. Seeds from a hybrid, however, will not produce another good quality hybrid. Only seeds created by cross-fertilizing purebred parents will produce a good quality hybrid.

Cross-fertilization

Purebred parent A The male flower is cut off the plant. This prevents the plant from pollinating itself.

Purebred parent B Pollen is collected in a bag and used to pollinate parent A.

Seed for hybrid

Self-pollination

Hybrid Bigger than parents and produces more grain.

What we eat Cob produced by the hybrid.

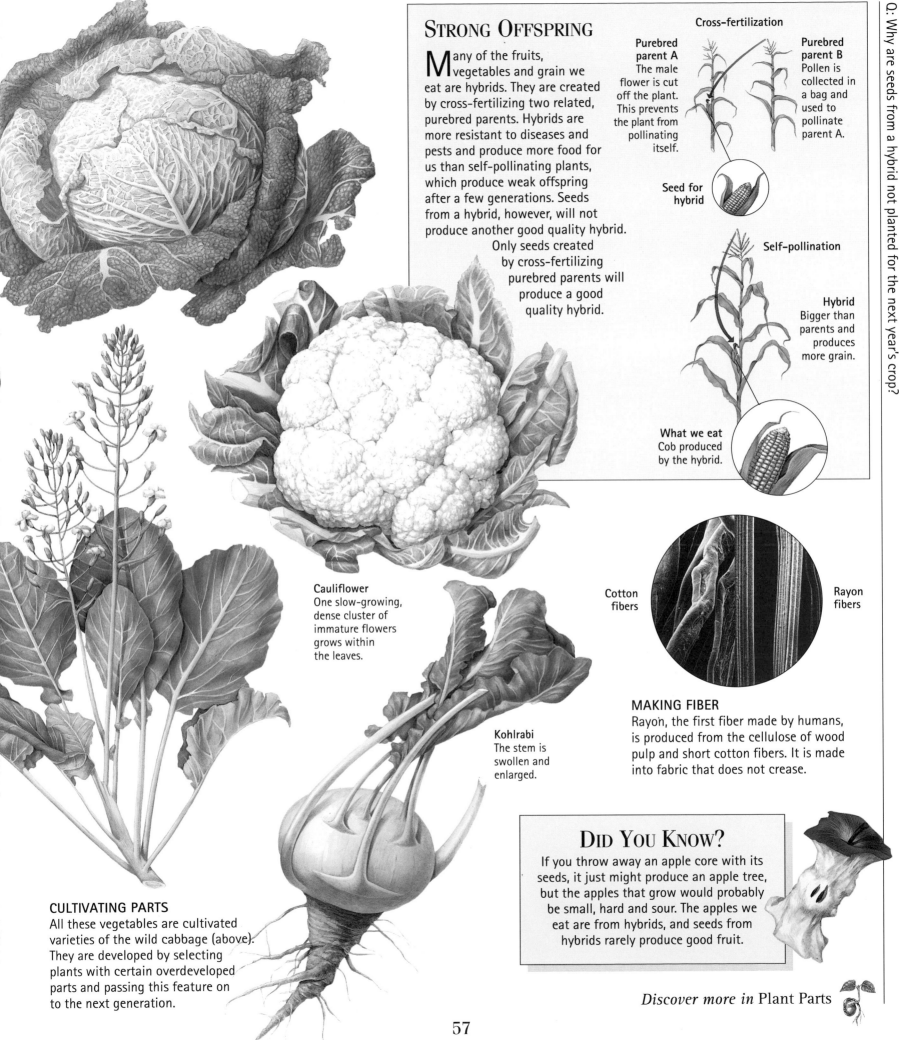

Cauliflower One slow-growing, dense cluster of immature flowers grows within the leaves.

Kohlrabi The stem is swollen and enlarged.

Cotton fibers

Rayon fibers

MAKING FIBER
Rayon, the first fiber made by humans, is produced from the cellulose of wood pulp and short cotton fibers. It is made into fabric that does not crease.

CULTIVATING PARTS
All these vegetables are cultivated varieties of the wild cabbage (above). They are developed by selecting plants with certain overdeveloped parts and passing this feature on to the next generation.

DID YOU KNOW?
If you throw away an apple core with its seeds, it just might produce an apple tree, but the apples that grow would probably be small, hard and sour. The apples we eat are from hybrids, and seeds from hybrids rarely produce good fruit.

Discover more in Plant Parts

57

PLANT DENSITY

Plants are necessary for life on Earth. By comparing present and future chlorophyll maps we can monitor plant density. On this map areas of highest chlorophyll are dark green on land and red to yellow in the sea. Pale yellow (on land) and pink (in the sea) indicate lowest densities.

STORING FOR THE FUTURE

Wild plants, cultivated plants and scientifically developed plant varieties are kept for the future. Seeds are stored in airtight packages or frozen in liquid nitrogen. Plants that do not have seeds, such as potatoes, can be stored as cuttings in laboratories, as shown here.

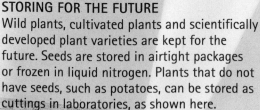

• PLANTS AND HUMANS •

Future Plants

Plants in the future, with the aid of genetic engineering, are likely to produce larger quantities or more nutritious foods and be better able to resist pests and diseases. New medicines may also come from future plants. As plant fossil fuels such as coal and oil run out, plants may provide alternative, safer and less polluting sources of energy. Plants may even hold the secrets for measuring and solving environmental pollution. But to use plants in the future we must avoid repeating the mistakes of the past. Many plant species have become extinct since the Stone Age, as land was cleared and wild plants were discarded in favor of large cultivated crops of only one species. What knowledge we might have gained from these plants is lost forever. Today, scientists can preserve a greater variety of plant species and genes. These are crucial for our future needs and research.

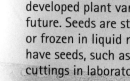

FUTURE PESTICIDES

Toxic pesticides, sprayed on crops, can badly affect animals and humans. Scientists have implanted a gene, from a bacterium that kills pest caterpillars, into experimental cotton plants. The leaves now produce the plant's own pesticide, which is not toxic to animals or to humans.

DID YOU KNOW?

Cars in some parts of America fill up their tanks with an alcohol called ethanol that is mixed with gasoline. Ethanol is produced by distilling fermented sugar from sugar cane and may become more widely used in the future.

VACCINE SEARCH
In the future, plant vaccines may stop the spread of new and fatal diseases. A common virus from cowpea plants has now been "mixed" with the HIV virus. An AIDS vaccine, produced from virus particles on the leaves, has been tested successfully on mice.

NATURAL HABITAT
Traditional farmers cultivate their crops, such as yams, where wild crops still grow. They provide a natural gene bank with greater genetic variety because genes flow between wild plants and their cultivated relatives.

BIODIVERSITY

Fields of grains, fruit orchards and managed forests are not natural environments. Only one species of plant grows, and any other species is either weeded out or has little opportunity to grow. In a natural environment, many different plant species share the same habitat and attract different wildlife. This natural variety of plant and animal species is called biodiversity. Other plants are now grown around cultivated crops to provide windbreaks, prevent soil erosion and attract—or distract—wildlife that would otherwise eat the crops. Biodiversity may be the way of the future.

POLLUTION INDICATORS
Lichens (above) are extremely sensitive to air pollution, especially sulfur dioxide. The lack of lichens in and around cities is a fairly reliable indicator of high pollution levels. Too many duckweeds or blue-green algae usually indicate water pollution.

Discover more in Food Plants

What Tree is That?

All trees have some things in common. They are perennial, which means they live and grow for many years, and they use seeds to reproduce. The trunks of trees, except those of palms, grow thicker and stronger every year. But it is the differences among trees that help us to identify them. Conifers, most of which have evergreen needle-shaped leaves, have no flowers and grow seeds inside cones. Broad-leaved trees are mostly deciduous, and all of them flower and grow seeds inside fruits. Within these two major groups, there are many types of tree. The shape of the tree, the patterns on the bark, the leaves, the cones, and the seeds (or flowers and fruits) can all be used to identify a tree or the genus to which it belongs. On these pages are 14 common trees, which are typical of their genera.

Moreton Bay Fig
(Ficus macrophylla)

FIGS
The flowers are hidden inside the fig, which resembles a ball with an opening at the top. Rings around the twigs are formed when the leaf sheaths, which protect the bud, break off.

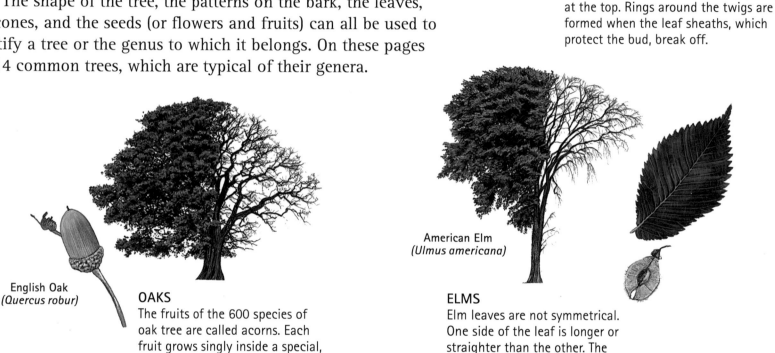

English Oak
(Quercus robur)

OAKS
The fruits of the 600 species of oak tree are called acorns. Each fruit grows singly inside a special, easily recognizable cup.

American Elm
(Ulmus americana)

ELMS
Elm leaves are not symmetrical. One side of the leaf is longer or straighter than the other. The seeds have two broad wings.

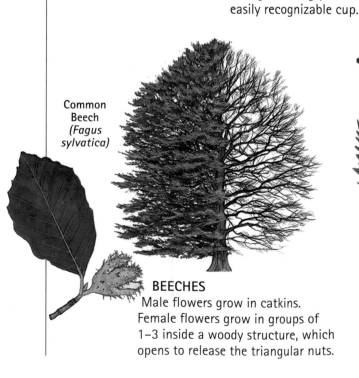

Common Beech *(Fagus sylvatica)*

BEECHES
Male flowers grow in catkins. Female flowers grow in groups of 1–3 inside a woody structure, which opens to release the triangular nuts.

Silver Birch *(Betula pendula)*

BIRCHES
Birches have condensed spikes of separate male and female flowers, known as catkins. Fruiting female catkins look like small cones.

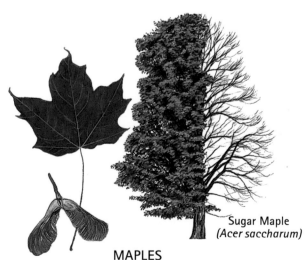

Sugar Maple *(Acer saccharum)*

MAPLES
Maple leaves have distinct lobes or divisions. Seeds have two wings that break into single wings as they fall.

Atlas Cedar
(Cedrus atlantica)

Monterey Pine
(Pinus radiata)

Balsam Fir
(Abies balsamea)

CEDARS
Needle-like leaves grow in clusters of up to 20 on dwarf shoots but are not held together by a sheath like pine needles. The cones break up after the seeds are shed.

PINES
Pine needles grow in groups of 2–5, held together by a sheath at the base of a dwarf shoot. Each pine branch has a number of needle-bearing, dwarf shoots.

FIRS
Fir cones stand upright on the branches and break up after shedding their seeds. Flattened leaves grow directly from branches, not on dwarf shoots.

Coastal She-oak
(Casuarina equisetifolia)

Southern Blue Gum
(Eucalyptus bicostata)

CASUARINAS
A flowering tree with unique leaves that are fused to small branches except for the leaftips (left), which resemble whorls of colorless or brown teeth.

GUM TREES
Different species of gum tree or eucalypt have distinctive bark patterns. Each flower has a lid that comes off to allow insects, birds or mammals to reach the nectar or pollen.

Senegal Date Palm
(Phoenix reclinata)

Lawson Cypress
(Chamaecyparis lawsoniana)

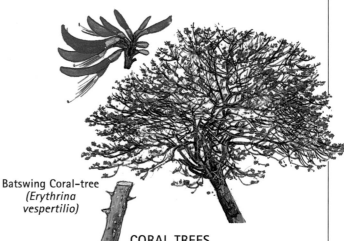

Batswing Coral-tree
(Erythrina vespertilio)

FEATHER-LEAVED PALMS
Each leaf is like a feather, made up of a number of segments that grow along a single main vein. The trees have no bark.

FALSE CYPRESSES
Small scalelike leaves grow in pairs, opposite each other, on green side branches. Female cones become soft as they mature.

CORAL TREES
These trees have prickly bark. Flowers have one large, folded red petal and several smaller, less obvious petals.

Glossary

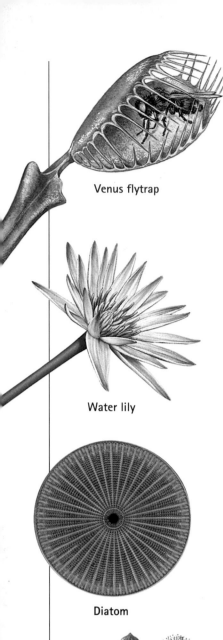

Venus flytrap

Water lily

Diatom

Eucalypt flowers

Dandelion

aerial roots Roots that absorb water from the air.

algae Simple plants that grow in water, have no true roots, stems or leaves but do manufacture their own food through photosynthesis.

annuals Plants that complete their life cycle— that is, germinate, grow to maturity, disperse their seeds and die— within a single year.

anther The part of the stamen (male reproductive organ) that produces pollen.

bract Modified leaf, often small but sometimes large and brightly colored, at the base of a flower.

bulb Condensed, and usually underground, stem and leaves in which the plant's food reserves are stored.

carbon dioxide Gas absorbed by plants during photosynthesis and given out by plants, animals and humans during respiration.

carpel The female seed-bearing organ of a flowering plant, which contains the stigma (on a stalk or style) and the ovary.

cell The basic unit or structure from which all plants and animals are made. Each microscopic cell has a special function or purpose.

cellulose Carbohydrate in plant cell walls that makes them strong and rigid.

chlorophyll A green pigment in special plant cells that absorbs energy from sunlight for use in photosynthesis (food making).

chloroplasts Structures within plant cells that contain the green chlorophyll.

conifers A group of mostly evergreen trees that produce seeds inside cones and usually have thin needle-shaped or scaly leaves.

cultivated Deliberately planted, tended and harvested by humans rather than growing wild.

deciduous Shedding, or dropping, leaves usually in autumn, winter or dry season. A deciduous tree is bare in the resting season and grows new leaves in the growing season.

dormant Not growing but resting or waiting for more suitable growing conditions.

embryo In plants, the stage after the female cell inside the ovule has been fertilized until the plant sprouts, or germinates.

epiphyte A plant that grows on trees and makes its own food. An epiphyte absorbs mineral salts from the surface of the tree and moisture from the air.

evergreen Having leaves all year round. An evergreen tree sheds its leaves throughout the year, instead of in a particular season, so it is never bare.

fibrous roots Roots that arise from nodes of the stem and not from a tap root.

fungus An organism, neither plant nor animal, that cannot make its own food so feeds on live or dead plant and animal tissue. Fungi break down and decompose plant and animal materials.

gamete Mature sex cell, either a male sperm or female egg.

gametophyte A tiny plant with male and female sex cells, or gametes. It is produced by spores, which have no sex cells.

gene The part in a cell that determines an inherited characteristic, passed on from previous generations. Genetic engineering can insert genes from one organism into another.

germination The stage in the life cycle when the stem and roots of a new plant sprout from a seed.

haustoria Special growths, or roots, used by parasitic plants to attach themselves to a host plant and feed on its food and water supply.

holdfast An attachment at the base of water plants such as algae that holds on to rocks. Like the rest of the plant, it absorbs water and minerals.

host The plant on which a parasite lives and feeds.

hybrid A plant produced by cross-fertilizing the female cell of one plant with the male cell of a related, but different, plant.

hyphae Threadlike cells that make up the body of a fungus.

mineral salts Salts from metals and rocks that are present in the soil and absorbed by plant roots. Salts contain nitrogen, phosphorous, magnesium, iron, potassium, calcium and other elements.

nectar Sugary liquid produced in special glands in flowers to attract insects, birds and mammals as pollinators.

node Position on plant stem from which new leaves, shoots and sometimes roots grow.

nutrients Substances that are needed to maintain life. Plant nutrients include mineral salts (usually from soil) and sugars (from photosynthesis).

ovary In plants, the part of the flower that contains the ovules. After pollination the ovary forms the fruit.

ovule The part of the plant that contains the female cell. After fertilization the ovule develops into a seed.

parasite A plant or fungus that lives and feeds on another living plant, and often damages or destroys it in the process.

perennials Plants that continue to live and grow for several, or many, years.

petal The second layer in the flower. It is usually colored and attracts pollinators.

pharmacology The science or study of drugs, including those derived from plants, and how they act on the human body.

phloem Tissue containing tubes of living cells that transport nutrients such as sugars and mineral salts from one part of the plant to another.

photosynthesis The process by which plants produce their own nutrients, in the form of sugars, using daylight, chlorophyll, mineral salts, water and carbon dioxide. Plants give off oxygen during photosynthesis.

phytoplankton Microscopic plants (usually algae) that drift or float in water.

pollen Minute grains produced in flowers or cones that contain the male sex cells, or gametes.

pollination The transfer of male pollen to the female stigma, which usually requires the help of pollinators such as the wind, insects or birds.

propagate To grow a new plant from the seeds, stems, rhizomes or roots of a parent plant.

purebred In plants, a plant produced when male pollen fertilizes a female stigma in the same flower, on the same plant or on a plant of the same variety and species.

reproduction The production of offspring or new plants from two different sex cells (sexual reproduction), or by methods such as cell division that do not require sex cells (asexual reproduction).

respiration The conversion of sugars into energy for growth, using oxygen and releasing carbon dioxide and water.

rhizome Underground stem that looks like a root (but it is not) and grows horizontally, or parallel, to the ground. Rhizomes in some plants are food stores and in many produce new plants.

sap The juice, made up of water, sugars and minerals, inside the stem of a plant.

sapling A young tree or shrub.

seedling A very young plant grown from a seed.

self-pollination The transfer of male pollen to a female stigma in the same flower or in a separate flower on the same plant. Self-pollination tends to produce weak plants after a few generations.

sporangia Cases or capsules that produce spores in plants such as mosses and ferns.

spore In plants, a reproductive cell that does not contain sex cells, or gametes, but is able to grow into a new plant called a gametophyte.

stamen The male part of a flower, containing a stalk with an anther, that produces pollen.

stigma The sticky tip of the stalk (style) in a flower's female reproductive organ, which receives the male pollen.

stolon A horizontal stem, that grows along and above the ground. New plants can grow from the nodes of the stolon where it touches the ground.

stomata Tiny holes, usually on the underside of leaves, through which gases and water vapor enter and exit. The stomata close at night or in very hot conditions.

tap root The first seedling root that may become the main root of the plant.

tendril A thin appendage on a climbing plant that coils around and clings to a support.

textile plant A plant with fibers that are woven into materials called textiles.

transpiration The movement of water from the roots to the stem and leaves and through the open holes, or stomata, into the atmosphere.

xylem Tissue containing tubes of dead cells that carry water and mineral salts up from the roots, through the stem, to the leaves.

Thistles

Drip tip leaf

Roses

Cactus

Conifer seeds

63

Index